PATRIK IAN M

THE 5 PILLARS OF
MENTAL
PERFORMANCE

99 TECHNIQUES &. HACKS
TO WIN IN LIFE BY TRAINING YOUR MIND

© Copyright 2023 - All rights reserved.

The content contained within this book may not be reproduced, duplicated, or transmitted without direct written permission from the author or the publisher.

Under no circumstances will any blame or legal responsibility be held against the publisher, or author, for any damages, reparation, or monetary loss due to the information contained within this book, either directly or indirectly.

Legal Notice:

This book is copyright protected. It is only for personal use. You cannot amend, distribute, sell, use, quote, or paraphrase any part of this book's content without the author's or publisher's consent.

Disclaimer Notice:

Please note that the information contained within this document is for educational and entertainment purposes only. All effort has been executed to present accurate, up-to-date, reliable, and complete information. No warranties of any kind are declared or implied. Readers acknowledge that the author does not render legal, financial, medical, or professional advice. The content within this book has been derived from various sources. Please consult a licensed professional before attempting any techniques outlined in this book.

By reading this document, the reader agrees that under no circumstances is the author responsible for any direct or indirect losses incurred as a result of the use of the information contained within this document, including, but not limited to, errors, omissions, or inaccuracies.

Table of Contents

Introduction 7

Pillar 1: Foundation 9

Chapter 1: The Essentials of Cognitive Performance 13
    Definition 13
    Mental Performance in Sports 14
    Mental Performance in Daily Life 17

Pillar 2: Thoughts 21

Chapter 2: Understanding Your Thoughts 25
    The Two Thought Processes 26
    Significance of Understanding Your Thoughts 29
    How to Understand Your Thoughts 31

Chapter 3: Thoughts and Emotions 37
    What Are Emotions? 37
    How Thoughts Impact Emotions 39
    Negative Thought Pattern 42

Chapter 4: Controlling Thoughts and Emotions 53
    Focus 53

Positive Thinking 55

Visualization 58

Meditation 60

Pillar 3: Emotional Agility 63

Chapter 5: Learning Emotional Agility 67

What is Emotional Agility? 67

Understanding Emotions 70

Chapter 6: How to Build Emotional Agility 77

Managing Your Emotions 77

Expressing Emotions in a Healthy Way 83

Chapter 7: Four Steps to Emotional Agility 87

Showing Up 87

Stepping Out 88

Walking Your 'Why' 89

Moving On 91

Pillar 4: Mindsets 93

Chapter 8: Exploring Mindsets 97

What is a Mindset? 97

The Impact, Importance, and Effects of Mindsets 97

Two Types of Mindsets 98

Chapter 9: Growth Mindset 103

What Does Having a Growth Mindset Mean? 103

Benefits of Having a Growth Mindset 104

How to Develop a Growth Mindset 106

Pillar 5: Mental Toughness 109

Chapter 10: What is Mental Toughness? 113

    Definition 113

    Benefits of Mental Toughness 115

    4 C's Model of Mental Toughness 116

Chapter 11: Mental Conditioning 123

    Mental Conditioning and Your Inner Strength 124

    Resilience 127

    Mental Flexibility 129

Chapter 12: How to Build Mental Toughness 131

    Connect to Your 'Why' 131

    Let Go of Self-Limiting Beliefs 133

    Overcoming Self-Doubt and Negative Self-Talk 134

    Visualization 135

Conclusion 137

Glossary 139

References 141

Introduction

Improving oneself is something we all aspire towards. Despite that, we often overlook the one thing that can make all the difference: our mind. Imagine unlocking its full potential and operating it more efficiently than ever before. Likely, helplessness and overwhelm will be replaced by self-actualization. Goal attainment will become an everyday occurrence. Procrastination and fear of failure will be relegated to the past. Thus, the possibilities are endless once you harness your mind's potential. With this book, you can revolutionize your life and elevate your mental power.

Cognitive performance, command of thought, emotional agility, a growth mindset, and mental toughness are the five pillars of this book. Learning these topics will present a different perspective on how the mind works. As such, adopting a growth mindset can transform your emotions and thoughts into assets when facing challenges. With greater mental discipline, you can improve your self-perception. The book also includes actionable steps for the practical implementation of these ideas. Hence, allowing you to cultivate further and strengthen your mental abilities.

Given my lifelong passion for mind exploration, I have dedicated myself to researching and analyzing the brain's functions. My time is spent reading white papers, conducting research, and reviewing peer-reviewed journals related to neuroscience and psychology. Throughout this journey, I have gained a deep understanding of how to hone the mind's capabilities. Thereby training countless individuals to develop their mental toughness.

This book is an elegant solution to sharing my knowledge with the world. A foundation is laid about what mental performance is as the first pillar. Only when you understand how your mind will function at optimum level will you know what you can achieve. With the second pillar, thoughts and emotions are broken down. When your thoughts are under control, they cannot drag you into a mess that slows you down. The third pillar comprehensively expounds upon emotional agility. Answering questions about your values provides a gauge to measure your emotions. This self-perception makes you a more capable player in the game of life.

Besides that, the fourth pillar of this book covers a growth mindset. Once you gain personal growth, your brain's capacity will likely improve. Lastly, under the final chapter are the wisdom into mental toughness. Use it to condition your mind to overcome adversity. You will find 99 techniques, tips, and strategies on how to be resilient in the face of opposition is how you will bring your visions to fruition peppered throughout the entire book. It's intentionally designed this way to serve as your guide along each step of the process. With these five pillars in my life, I have achieved peak performance. Likewise, I overcame challenges that once seemed unconquerable. Life has never been better.

Use this book to experience the same benefits I have regarding ruggedness in overcoming setbacks. Begin taking charge of your mental performance, thoughts, emotions, personal growth, and toughness. Bring down the challenges you face using your newfound power and the tools and principles provided. Lastly, take advantage of the grit and potential inside of you to accomplish your goals.

Pillar 1:
Foundation

The human mind differentiates us from animals based on our unique thought processes. Our personalities and skill sets reflect the exertion of our mental faculties. Through the first pillar, discover the foundation of cognitive performance. Understanding this cornerstone will unlock your mind's potential, enabling you to achieve results. This pillar also provides the groundwork for our exploration of mental performance. Subsequently, creating a solid footing for your journey to optimize your cognitive abilities.

Chapter 1:
The Essentials of Cognitive Performance

Success in our personal, social, and work lives hinges on our mental performance. Achieving an optimal level of mental performance is a complex subject that needs more in-depth exploration. Considering this, the following chapter will explore mental performance and its relevance to you.

Definition

Mental performance refers to the efficiency of our cognitive functioning and ability to execute our intentions. As individuals, we naturally all aspire to reach our utmost potential in our responses and intellectual prowess. Our mental performance measures the extent to which we achieve this goal. A sharp and active mind can analyze situations thoroughly, use the information to perform better, and increase the chances of success. Achieving this level of mental performance elevates us beyond average.

In achieving this level of mental performance, mastering all your learning and observation faculties is required. These faculties include attention, perception, reasoning, memory, habits, and intuition. Memory and habits, for instance, operate in the unconscious mind, which is not directly accessible to our consciousness. Nonetheless, such faculties can be trained and harnessed to support our conscious ambitions.

Mental Performance in Sports

While participating in sports, athletes face demands not only on physical but also on mental abilities. Meeting these demands distinguishes them from being great sports figures to excellent athletes. Hence, the life of an A-list sports star is often marked by stress, stemming from public scrutiny to fulfilling professional obligations. To succeed in such an environment, athletes must develop mental fortitude beyond coping.

Handling the pressure of making mistakes is one mental challenge that athletes face. Unfortunately, what sometimes shapes this pressure in an athlete's mindset is coaching. Some coaches reinforce winning at all costs and condemn failure. For example, when a coach does not offer constructive criticism and highlights only the mistakes, athletes fear making any errors. Consequently, it sets a high-performance standard that promotes a culture of fear instead of growth.

Combating this negative mindset requires reframing our thoughts around failure. Instead of seeing it as a setback, view it as an opportunity for growth and learning. Likewise, we should understand that failure is an inevitable part of growth and does not define someone's worth. Focus also on the progress rather than the results and celebrate small wins. Alternatively, practice self-compassion and treat yourself with kindness and understanding, even in the face of failure. By adopting a growth mindset and focusing on learning, anyone can overcome the fear of failure and achieve their full potential.

Another challenge for athletes is maintaining self-care. Unfortunately, many people ignore their self-care needs out of a misguided belief that it implies weakness. However, taking simple steps to de-stress can make a difference. As such, soaking in a hot bath is a great way to unwind after a long, hectic day. The warm water helps soothe your body, which helps calm your mind. As your body temperature rises in the water, you will naturally feel a sense of relaxation and tranquility. Additionally, a hot bath can be a great way to relieve muscle tension and soreness. Besides that, relaxing your mind and body at the end of the day improves sleep, preparing you mentally for the new day. Waking up well-rested will bring the energy you need to put forward an A-game.

Many athletes struggle with performance anxiety at some point, as nobody likes the unpleasant feeling of underperformance. Physical symptoms accompany this anxiety, such as sweaty hands, an elevated heart rate, and a strange feeling in the stomach. Related mental symptoms include overthinking and an inward focus. Nonetheless, coping strategies can help alleviate the pressure of performance anxiety. For instance, seeking therapy helps athletes with performance anxiety in several ways. First, therapy helps identify the thoughts, emotions, and behaviors contributing to this anxiety. With this awareness, athletes can learn coping skills and strategies for managing their anxiety and improving their performance. Additionally, therapy helps develop a greater sense of self-awareness, which can improve overall well-being.

Unfortunately, the stigma around getting counseling in the sports community prevents some from reaching out for it. Athletes may worry that admitting to struggling with mental health concerns could harm their careers. Consequently, reports show that 5% to 31% of athletes use performance-enhancing drugs *(Malva, 2018)*. Then, around 13.5%

of athletes have eating disorders due to dealing with body pressures *(Sundgot-Borgen & Torstveit, 2004)*. Some categories have a higher percentage, with women in aesthetic sports having a 42% chance of getting an eating disorder. Yet, to combat these concerns, an athlete needs to reframe therapy as a tool for enhancing their performance. Remember that mental health is just as important as physical health.

There are many alternative approaches to improving one's mental health. Yet, they may not be as effective as therapy, but they can still be beneficial. For instance, music can be an effective relaxation technique to bring calmness. Find some songs you enjoy, sit on a bench, and enjoy the scenic atmosphere while listening to them. Moreover, mindfulness techniques, like meditation or tai chi, can help eliminate stress and promote well-being. Breathing techniques can also help reduce anxiety. One such technique is lying on your back and inhaling until your belly rises, followed by a slow exhalation. Repeating this a few times can help you feel at ease.

Another way to improve mental focus is by visualizing victory before a game. This allows your mind to remain fixed on the goal and helps cut distractions so that you perform your best. Alternatively, visualize what you want in a high-pressure situation, like the start of an important game. Picture the obstacles you will face and how to overcome them. Stay driven by repeating positive affirmations throughout the game. By remaining in the present, you will be aware of potential threats, allowing you to bypass them. These steps of visualization, positive affirmations, and staying in the present will increase your focus and self-control.

To excel in high-pressure situations, athletes must overcome various forms of stress. Therefore, achieving mental focus is crucial to overcoming these challenges. As such, poor mental health harms an athlete's performance. Meanwhile, taking a holistic approach to mental health involves examining sources of stress both on and off the field. Approaches mentioned above, such as therapy, can help improve mental health and build resilience. This improved mental health can give athletes the toughness they need to succeed against tough opponents.

Mental Performance in Daily Life

The interdependence between executive and cognitive functions regulates our daily lives. Executive functions refer to the higher-level cognitive abilities that help us to manage, control, and organize our thoughts and actions. Meanwhile, cognitive functions encompass the mental processes that enable us to learn, remember, perceive, and think. In daily challenges, executive functions help us to control our cognitive faculties, allowing us to adjust our behavior to fit the situation. For instance, when faced with a deadline, we may have to adjust our routine and wake up early to complete the task on time. This requires us to estimate the time to meet the deadline and plan our schedule accordingly. Likewise, being flexible and resisting the urge to catch extra sleep demonstrates our ability to practice inhibitory control.

As such, inhibitory control allows us to resist impulses and stay focused, preventing distractions from hindering productivity. Learning to say no and ignoring external pressures can be critical to success. Additionally, inhibitory control helps us avoid getting sidetracked by irrelevant external stimuli that could deter us from our goals. To practice inhibitory control, you may do the following:

- **Prioritize.** Identify your top priorities and focus your energy on those tasks. Resist the urge to take on additional obligations that may distract you from reaching your goals.

- **Create boundaries.** Establish boundaries around your time, space, and resources. For example, use a *"do not disturb"* feature on your phone or email when focusing on a specific task.

- **Delay gratification.** Learn to postpone immediate gratification in favor of long-term rewards. As such, resist the urge to check social media or email during work hours and instead schedule specific times.

- **Be mindful.** Practice mindfulness techniques such as deep breathing or meditation. This can help you develop greater self-awareness and control over your thoughts and emotions.

Furthermore, reasoning is a crucial executive function. As such, it allows us to identify similarities and differences between things. Determining how something compares with something else lets you make better evaluations. An example of this is when you are comparing job candidates. They both have similar qualifications, employment histories, and employment equity profiles. Spotting the similarities and differences between the two candidates allows you to determine who should get the job offer.

Meanwhile, to effectively manage multiple activities, you need to practice *"branching."* This involves focusing your mind on the current task. Yet, keeping the other undertakings in your periphery to alert you if any require immediate attention. Prioritize tasks by focusing on the most crucial ones first and then addressing less urgent ones. With this approach, you cut stressors and achieve greater productivity in your daily routine. Alternatively, actioning two things simultaneously is called *'dual execution.'* For instance, taking notes while listening to a lecture is an example of dual execution. In dual execution, you focus on both duties attentively, leveraging different faculties without losing focus. However, it is unwise to multitask beyond your capacity because your progress may slow down when your attention is dispersed.

Decision-making is another challenging executive function, as it often demands certainty. Regardless, it is much easier once you understand how to make decisions, even with limited information. To make a choice, begin by exploring all available options when confronted with a problem, situation, or course of action. Use your prediction, imagination, and planning skills to evaluate the potential consequences of each option. Likewise, consider the possible outcomes. Then, based on your analysis, decide on the best path forward.

Along with the other necessary executive functions comes planning. Planning incorporates creativity by imagining and interacting with variables to determine desired outcomes. Effective planning requires determining your goals first. After this, work out the steps to achieve that purpose. There will likely be multiple ways to achieve it. Thus, planning requires determining which course of action will be most effective. The most effective path will generate the most success with the lowest expenditure of resources.

Effective time estimation is closely related to several other executive functions, such as observation and prediction. To accurately estimate how long a particular activity will take, carefully track its progress. Tracking helps, especially when working with a tight schedule. Likewise, develop the ability to predict the time required for each task. Then, adjusting your pace to meet the deadline will set you apart as a highly skilled and efficient professional. Also, an excellent sense of time management is essential to success in any field.

Lastly, working memory is essential in almost any occupation. It consists of retaining information about the important tasks you are doing now. Smoothly switching to the next task on our priority list is the upshot of this ability. Discarding inconsequential information is another consequence. Keep relevant information in mind for a logical flow to your next task.

Pillar 2: Thoughts

The thoughts we have lead to the actions we do. When your thoughts are in a positive space that drives you to achieve, the rest of you will respond accordingly. In this section, we will explore thoughts and how you can understand them better.

Chapter 2:
Understanding Your Thoughts

The first question is, *"What is the definition of a thought?"* Many people have debated its meaning. Simply put, a thought is an electrochemical message in the brain *(Dougherty, 2011)*. Electrochemical messages consist of electrical and chemical impulses that carry messages between nerves. Think of it like a signal moving along a telephone line or the chemicals in a battery producing charge.

Thoughts may also pertain to stimuli you have observed in your surroundings, such as the sound of traffic or the smell of the pizza you eat. They might come from an internal message you have generated based on your inner world. For example, an internal stimulus could be a memory of your first job or a feeling about someone you are meeting.

Besides that, thoughts contain meaning, patterns, language, perceptions, and other significances. They interpret what is happening, guiding us about what we should do next. While human thought and its origins remain a complex and ongoing subject of study, much has already been explored. To begin with, it is essential to understand the different types of thought processes that occur.

The Two Thought Processes

According to the Dual Process Theory, humans think in two distinct ways. The first is fast and intuitive processing, which helps us think quickly and efficiently. Usually, this process is valuable when accomplishing tasks and coping with stressors. Meanwhile, the second process is deliberative and slow. As such, it involves a detailed examination of information to produce more accurate results. Both processing types are essential depending on our daily needs.

Implicit or Automatic Thinking Processes

A *"gut feeling"* is an example of the outcome of an implicit thinking process. For instance, imagine a baker who senses the need to check on the oven. The driving force for this gut feeling could be the smell of something burning. Likely, the baker may not consciously link the odor with the need to check on the confection. Yet, the implicit process carries this intuitive decision to prevent potential problems such as overbaking.

Meanwhile, when encountering new people, we often make snap judgments about them. In seconds, our brain combines the information we observe, such as their appearance and accent, with our past experiences to form an attitude toward the person. For instance, if we have had positive experiences with people with similar characteristics, we will likely have a positive attitude toward this new person. This fast and automatic thinking process is necessary to navigate the world and make decisions efficiently. However, it is essential to recognize that our snap judgments may not always be accurate or fair. Hence, remain open-minded to re-evaluate our attitude toward others based on further information and interactions.

Besides that, confidence comes from making the best decision possible with the information available. Data quality can improve our choices, but our automatic thinking process can provide us with the most accurate result, even with limited data. However, our perception of the *"right"* decision may change based on our reflection on past actions, especially when not stressed. Yet, maintain confidence that you did your best given the circumstances.

Altogether, the automatic thinking process often revolves around pre-trained responses from past experiences and knowledge. These subconscious actions can be beneficial in situations that require quick and decisive actions, such as shifting a car to avoid hitting a child on the road. In these critical moments, we must act fast, even if it means potentially damaging another vehicle, to prevent harm or loss of life.

On the other hand, the controlled thinking process is better suited for situations that do not require immediate action. In such cases, it takes time to consider all the information, weigh the pros and cons, and make a deliberate decision.

Explicit or Controlled Thinking Processes

When we have a lot of data to grasp, we engage in controlled thinking. A good example of this is a student who is working through a textbook for an examination. They analyze large quantities of information to better understand the subject at hand. According to Fabio et al. (2019), controlled thinking allows us to use mental flexibility by examining multiple points of view. Adapting our mindset and knowledge base on a topic gives us a solid foundation to vindicate a tough decision.

Controlled thinking is necessary when making value-based judgments, where decisions are based on personal beliefs. As such, it enables individuals to evaluate different options, ensuring their choices align with their values. Additionally, it helps provide reasonable explanations for these decisions when faced with challenging situations with no clear-cut answer. Failing to use controlled thinking may lead to hasty decisions that do not align with an individual's values, resulting in confusion and potential issues. However, controlled thinking can be speculative and reflective and may not always lead to high certainty. Despite this, it remains critical to make informed decisions that align with personal beliefs.

Nevertheless, controlled and automatic thinking helps equally. Using them when needed enables us to respond appropriately to all situations. For instance, automatic thinking is useful for situations where there is no time for contemplation. Meanwhile, controlled thinking allows us to overcome biases, examine different perspectives, and make informed decisions.

Lawyers are a good example of individuals who must use automatic and controlled thinking when appropriate. Lawyers sometimes have to think on their feet, such as when dealing with difficult clients or opponents who throw unexpected challenges. They must respond quickly and appropriately to these situations, or they may lose their reputation and business. Yet, there are also times when they must know every case detail, including the legal implications of what happened. In such situations, they must utilize a controlled thinking process to establish a broad understanding of the case.

Using automatic and controlled thinking enables us to respond appropriately to all circumstances. To get better at mastering thinking processes, recognize and manage different types of thoughts, as the following section will explain.

Significance of Understanding Your Thoughts

Most of our thoughts happen on an unconscious level. Suppressed memories, ingrained habits, and language abilities are just some of the things contained in our unconscious mind. Sometimes, the unconscious mind needs to be altered. Adjusting it is particularly important when exerting an unconscious negative influence, but this takes time and multiple techniques to change. The first step is to discern when your unconscious mind exerts itself and when you are consciously deciding something.

Understanding the operations of our unconscious mind and their influence on our thoughts is essential to understanding ourselves better. Subsequently, it clarifies our thought processes and how they affect our decisions, affirmations, and conclusions on a conscious level. Increased awareness of our emotions and triggers allows us to identify when we behave unintentionally. Recognizing these patterns can help determine when unconscious thoughts influence our behavior.

For example, slips of the tongue refer to situations when one says something they did not intend to. Usually, this situation happens because of a brief lapse in the thought process. These errors in speech can reveal how our unconscious mind processes information. Likewise, they provide insights into our mental state. As such, if someone accidentally refers to a friend by an ex-partner's name, it may indicate that they are still processing feelings related to that past relationship. Similarly, unintentionally using words associated with negative emotions may mean underlying stress or anxiety.

Moreover, being aware of your unconscious thoughts can help you in guiding your actions. For instance, holding onto childhood desires could be an unconscious thought that affects your decisions. By spotting this desire, you can assess if it aligns with your current goals and respond accordingly. Either change your career path or assert the dominance of your conscious desire and replace the former with a new aspiration.

As you encounter impulses stemming from your unconscious mind, take a moment to reflect and ask yourself a few questions. Suppose you want to purchase a new house on the market. Yet, your unconscious mind persists with thoughts like *"Find a better place."* In such a case, ask yourself, *"Is this expectation realistic?"* Considering your financial situation, you can evaluate if the impulse or desire is achievable. Then, questions like, *"How does this desire make me feel?"* and *"What emotions drive it?"* allow you to process your emotions' role in shaping your thoughts and desires. Identifying the emotions driving your desires creates an opportunity for introspection and self-reflection. This insight into your deeper motivations and underlying needs leads to clearer decision-making.

In uncertain situations, the fear of the unknown can be paralyzing. These fears act as a defense mechanism to prevent us from taking perceived risks. While it may be well-intentioned, this fear-induced hesitation can lead to missed opportunities. Yet, taking the time to understand our thoughts helps differentiate rational and irrational fears. Subsequently, it allows approaching the situation more objectively. For instance, start by exploring the reasons behind such fears. Then, question whether they are based on concrete evidence or simply our imagination.

An alternative perspective is a healthy approach to understanding your thoughts and breaking free from thinking habits. For example, a teacher faced with disengaged students can discuss their lesson plans with other educators to gain fresh perspectives and create more relatable lesson examples. Examining the best possible outcome can also break negative thought patterns and encourage action.

Determining the worst-case scenario can also put things into perspective and act as a moral compass. By exploring the best and worst outcomes, possibilities are clearly defined, and practical considerations are not overlooked. Seeking others' opinions and breaking down fixed points of view can also expand our understanding and increase our societal awareness.

Replacing negative urges with positive ones is a follow-up step to identifying and questioning unconscious thoughts. For example, replacing the urge to gamble with investing in a stock portfolio can provide a sense of unpredictability while creating a secure financial future. By understanding our thoughts and utilizing these questioning methods, we can gain clarity and further develop our critical thinking ability.

In the upcoming section, we will explore frames of mind and how they shape our thoughts. Expanding our knowledge of how thoughts work, we can continue developing our self-awareness and decision-making skills.

How to Understand Your Thoughts

Our minds are a hive of activity. Thoughts are flying around within our conscious sphere and beneath it. We can keep track of various things, focusing on multiple matters simultaneously. There are several mental factors present in our minds in addition to thoughts. These factors include memories, solutions, feelings, and ideas, amongst other things. It helps to understand the three frames of mind to simplify this concatenation of mental elements.

Frames of Mind

There are three frames of mind, such as *"engaged," "automatic,"* and *"analytic."* They all have a specific function intended to achieve a particular purpose. Engaged and automatic fall into implicit thinking, while analytic is under explicit thinking.

*Do you ever feel completely immersed in a task? Almost as if you are **"in the zone"** with little to no attention given to distractions or other thoughts?* In such situations, you are in the engaged frame of mind.

Under engagement requires the complete focus and attention of the individual. Hence, distractions are filtered out, and all attention is directed toward the task. Daydreams and other thoughts are relegated to the unconscious mind, ensuring uninterrupted concentration. Also, this frame of mind is most beneficial in reducing stress levels by allowing us to direct energy toward our priorities.

Engagement is not only conducive to productivity but also to healthy conversations. When someone demonstrates engagement, it indicates a keen interest in the other person's viewpoint, ensuring they feel heard. Imagine a friend sharing some exciting news about a new job opportunity. Being engaged would allow you to comprehend the whole picture without distractions. Consequently, making you understand their concerns better, provide empathy, and offer comfort.

The second frame of mind, known as automatic thinking, operates in the background of our mind. In this state, our thoughts flow effortlessly without conscious processing or effort. The implicit thinking process during automatic thinking drives our responses to various external stimuli. In essence, this instinctual perception of our environment triggers our next move and propels us to take actionable steps.

For example, dodging an oncoming vehicle is an act that seems reflexive. One moment you mind your business; the next, you are leaping out of the way, heart racing. But such reactions are due to automatic thinking, which handles the calibrated response to external stimuli. Almost instantly, the brain processes a series of factors. These may be the size, speed, and trajectory of the incoming vehicle, the visual and auditory clues available, and the presence (or absence) of possible escape routes. In the milliseconds it takes to complete this analysis, the brain sends the command to move, and you dart out of the way. Hence, our minds are astounding in reaching conclusions and developing action plans through automatic thinking.

However, our brains often fall prey to misinformation beyond our control. Subsequently, when automatic thinking is based on inaccurate data, it can lead us to irresponsible actions. An influential figure, for instance, which promotes shouting as an effective means of asserting authority, can influence our perception. Unfortunately, the validity of this idea goes unquestioned since, during automatic thinking, our brains rely on shortcuts and heuristics. These shortcuts can be helpful in daily life but can also be flawed and produce suboptimal outcomes. In the example of shouting to assert dominance, the underlying premise may seem valid because it was taught to us by someone respected. Our brains, therefore, do not question it because it requires less cognitive effort to adopt the behavior.

To combat this, reflection and examination of our thoughts are necessary to weed out unsound information. In implementing a filtration process for our automatic thoughts, follow these steps:

1. **Recognize your automatic thought.** Learn to identify the automatic thoughts in your mind in response to certain situations.

2. **Identify Cognitive Distortions.** Cognitive distortions are inaccurate beliefs that can lead to negative thinking patterns. Recognizing these patterns can bring them to your attention and challenge their validity.

3. **Develop Positive Self-Talk.** Positive self-talk is speaking to yourself in a positive and supportive manner. Develop a list of affirmations or positive statements to counter negative self-talk.

Past traumas and unpleasant experiences may also trigger automatic negative thinking. Fear and uncertainty can cloud our judgment, rendering our automatic thinking incapable of serving its protective function. To combat this, cognitive behavioral therapy is an excellent solution. Socratic dialogue is another remedy, providing a method to question conclusions or decisions critically. Alternatively, consider writing down recurring negative thoughts and examine them objectively. Then, reword these thoughts into more positive phrasing, which can help combat negativity.

Meanwhile, analytic thinking represents the third frame of mind and is an intentional process. As part of the explicit thinking process, you exercise direct control over it. Thus, analytic thinking empowers us to manipulate data to make informed decisions, even when faced with complex situations. Through this process, we examine evidence, experiences, and conditions while utilizing the information stored in our minds.

There are six subcategories of the analytical frame of mind, such as:

- **Observation.** The ability to perceive details, patterns, and relationships. This subcategory is crucial to the analytical frame of mind, as it enables one to gather data and form new insights.

In daily life, observation can be improved by attention to details that usually go unnoticed.

- **Reflection.** Involves thinking deeply about experiences and ideas. It is an effective problem-solving subcategory that evaluates different perspectives and considers possible solutions. Reflection also helps in decision-making by allowing us to weigh the pros and cons and consider long-term implications.

- **Generating Solutions.** Refers to thinking critically and creatively to create new solutions to problems. In execution, generating solutions turn abstract ideas into practical, measurable goals. This subcategory is essential in implementing decisions and identifying new opportunities.

- **Planning.** Process of creating a roadmap to achieve a goal. It is the subcategory that gives meaning and direction to the solutions generated. Moreover, it involves organizing resources, setting timelines, and identifying potential obstacles to implement solutions effectively. In personal growth and development, planning can be crucial in achieving objectives systematically.

- **Mental Performance.** The cognitive abilities required to maintain an analytical frame of mind. This includes concentration, memory retention, and multitasking. Improving mental performance can enhance productivity, creativity, and decision-making. Simple activities such as reading or brain teasers help improve mental performance.

- **Imagining.** Creating and visualizing scenarios and ideas. This subcategory is critical to creative thinking, enabling one to see beyond external limitations. Also, imagining helps develop new concepts, visualize solutions, and explore possibilities. Hence, leading to unconventional and innovative outcomes.

Focus on the observation subcategory to make the most of your analytical frame. When carefully perceiving details, patterns, and relationships, you can gather high-quality data and form new insights. The other subcategories, such as reflection, generating solutions, planning, mental performance, and imagining, build on the foundation of observation to create reliable results. Also note that the conclusions you draw using analytical thinking might not align with the findings you made using the other frames of mind. Dissimilar determinations produce *"cognitive dissonance,"* defined as mental inconsistencies causing you confusion. If this happens, review or reflect on your conclusion with the other frame of mind and determine how you need to alter it. Further, locate what caused the findings to differ.

However, do not overuse this third frame of mind, even though it leads to reliable results. As such, when we overanalyze a situation or problem, we become paralyzed by indecision or second-guess our initial conclusions. Not to mention, it will erode your confidence because you will continually be questioning yourself. Remember, all three frames of mind have their purpose and should get used. By understanding the meaning behind each and how they work, you will understand your mind better and how to use it to maximum benefit.

Chapter 3:
Thoughts and Emotions

As humans, our thoughts and emotions are an inseparable part of our lives. Some days, we may wake up feeling energized and ready to take on the world. Yet, on other days, we struggle to get out of bed. Sometimes, we are filled with contentment and love; at different times, we may feel overwhelmed by fear or sadness. Our thoughts and emotions can be likened to a wild rollercoaster ride that we all experience, regardless of our preferences. *But what exactly are thoughts and emotions, and why do they hold such power over us?*

What Are Emotions?

Emotions are the lens through which we experience the world around us, allowing us to flow feelings about ourselves, others, things, and conditions. For example, feeling proud of yourself for exhibiting self-control when led into temptation is an emotion that arises from an internal event. Meanwhile, boredom from waiting in an unmoving queue is an emotion resulting from external factors.

While we can respond to emotions differently, appropriate responses can be challenging when we do not understand the feelings we are experiencing. Building our emotional vocabulary is a solution to this phenomenon. This involves understanding the definitions for multiple levels of emotions and feelings, not just the overarching ones. Emotional vocabulary lists are available online, and you can easily access them with a quick search.

Emotions help us to bond with one another and reconcile differences of opinion. In fact, emotions are the determining factor for up to 90% of our decisions *(Natarelli, n.d.)*. Thus, you can use emotions to build understanding with others and bring your groups closer together. Then, emotional bonding is often the driving force behind community groups that strive to effect change. Even if you cannot find the right words to express your point, your emotions can help you convey them effectively.

Moreover, emotions are contagious, meaning people experience a similar emotional state as those around them. This principle of emotional contagion shows how emotions can be used as a tool of influence. For instance, ignoring a disgruntled employee will likely lead to others becoming disgruntled. On the other hand, talking with the employee and listening to their concerns will contribute to alleviating the situation. Hence, preventing others from being influenced into an agitated state.

Our cultural traditions and beliefs significantly influence how we express and handle our emotions. While some cultures consider it healthy to share your feelings openly, others encourage you to be reserved and *"be strong"* by hiding your emotions or keeping them to yourself. As such, in some Western cultures, it is considered healthy and honest to communicate your feelings, thoughts, and opinions to others. In contrast, in some Asian cultures, particularly in Japan, expressing negative emotions such as anger is considered impolite and can cause discomfort to others. Subsequently, the Japanese often strive for harmony and avoid confrontation. That said, they tend to suppress negative emotions and use indirect communication instead of confrontational.

Moreover, genetics also affect our emotions, and our genetic structure can affect how we react to them. For instance, some families are more open and love socializing. In contrast, others are more prim and proper and never show how they feel. Yet, this leads to awkward family gatherings where different branches of the family do not seem to connect.

Finally, physical conditions like brain tumors, cancer, Parkinson's disease, multiple sclerosis, and Alzheimer's can also impact our emotions. Thyroid disorders can cause our hormones to fluctuate, leading to varying emotional reactions. Meanwhile, metabolic diseases such as diabetes can cause our energy levels to fluctuate, influencing how we feel about something.

How Thoughts Impact Emotions

The way you think can alter the way you feel about things. In fact, our emotions are flexible by nature and influenced by both internal and external experiences. This includes our inner world, where our thoughts and feelings can interact. For example, if you find something ugly, such as a piece of art displayed, you might not feel enthusiastic about it. Conversely, our emotions can also affect the way we think about something. As such, a positive interaction with someone could make us put aside any negative thoughts about them since those pleasant vibes will override anything else. These interplay between thoughts and emotions are dynamic occurrences that influence how we go through our daily lives.

A dynamic relationship with our thoughts and feelings enables us to refine and transform our perspectives. Subsequently, our initial impressions of someone or something are not permanent. Hence, we can modify them as we gain fresh insights and information. Let us say, initially, you thought that a particular book was not worth reading based on the title and the cover. However, after reading reviews and recommendations from trusted people, you decide to give the book a chance. As you start reading, you realize the book has many valuable insights you had not considered before. Due to that, you begin to change your perspective on the book. This example demonstrates how a dynamic relationship works.

Using thoughts, you can also introspect on the emotions you have about someone. Overly harsh feelings can be sniffed out with observation and logic. Self-examination might amend your feelings toward them if your emotions were not well-founded.

The influence of our thoughts on our emotions can also manifest through our habits and personality traits. For example, suppose you habitually check the latest news on topics that interest you. In that case, you are more likely to feel emotionally invested in them. Conversely, if something does not typically pique your interest, you may not experience strong emotions. Additionally, your personality can also influence your emotional response. As such, extroverts may feel more comfortable and content in a social setting than introverts. Both habits and personality traits can lead to varying levels of attentiveness, affecting our emotional reactions. Generally, the more attentive we are to something, the greater its impact on our mood.

There are generally two ways to change an emotion, such as:

1. **Re-evaluation of your thoughts and feelings about the situation.** Involve introspection and considering different

perspectives. For instance, if you receive negative feedback on a project you have been working on, you might initially feel disappointed. However, upon reflection, you may realize some valid points in the feedback you can use to improve your work. Looking at the feedback from a different perspective allows you to re-evaluate your initial emotions. Consequently, leading to personal growth and development.

2. **Alteration of external stimuli.** Include changing your environment or circumstances to improve your emotional state. As such, moving to a company with a healthier attitude toward employees could be the solution if you are in an abusive job. Your work environment is a daily external stimulus, and changing it can elevate your emotional state toward your career.

Besides that, positivity researchers determined that 10% of your happiness depends on your circumstances in life. Then, 40% relies on things you decide to do to become happier, while 50% on your genetics *(Lyubormirsky, Schkade, & Sheldon, 2015)*. These statistics indicate that close to half (40%) of your happiness is directly within your grasp to change.

Cognitive Behavioral Therapy (CBT) is a powerful technique to enhance happiness. This therapy modifies your thinking patterns by informing you of negative thoughts and their recurrent cycles. As you change your automatic negative thinking, CBT positively influences you even when you are not conscious of it. Also, it allows you to increase your attention control and focus on the healthiest, most positive direction. CBT's most significant advantage is its long-term effects on your mental well-being.

"Affect labeling" is another technique to improve happiness and positivity. When you experience emotions, labeling them and stepping back to

evaluate the context and feeling state objectively can effectively provide precise details instead of vague feelings. By tracing the stimulus that triggered your emotion and having a clear title of what you feel, you can determine an appropriate action plan. In this way, you remain in control of the situation instead of feeling overwhelmed and confused.

Aside from these techniques, practicing forgiveness, kindness, gratitude, mindfulness, and positivity exercises help heal deteriorated relationships, including the ones with yourself. Building mindfulness can occur through various methods, such as meditation, breathing techniques, and visualization. You can enhance positive thinking by performing daily affirmations and visualizing yourself in a state of success or happiness.

Emotions help you manage situations and process what you experience. Yet, to make the most effective use of their healing quality, you should know that you control them and understand how your thoughts can affect them. Once you achieve this, you can use your emotions to positively impact your thoughts by altering negative thought patterns for the better. By employing these techniques and changing negative thought patterns, you can increase your happiness and transform your life positively.

Negative Thought Pattern

Negative thoughts can creep up on us and distort our perceptions of situations. But the reality may not be as bleak as our thoughts make it out to be. Knowing how negative thought patterns occur and the most common negative automatic thought patterns are essential to prevent inaccurate interpretation of information. In this way, we can identify when they occur and re-evaluate the situation to alter our observations to something more accurate.

Cognitive distortions are a subset of negative thought patterns. Distortions result in incorrect assumptions. These incorrect assumptions include being too critical of yourself and twists of reality. However, negative thought is not the same as negative thought patterns. The first is transient, while the latter is a way of thinking that puts everything in a worse light. As such, it makes good things bad while bad things are made worse.

This process can be destructive and affects mental health permanently if left unchecked for too long. And for someone who already struggles with mental health, the negative thinking process can drag you even lower—sometimes past your breaking point. As such, it is necessary to do what you can to snap that thought process and start seeing the positive things in your life and the neutral things for what they are. The best way to do this is to know the triggers for the negative thinking processes you may be using.

One of the ways thinking processes may come to hold sway in your life is the glorification of struggle. Pop culture, history, art, and literature all laud it. While overcoming difficulty and succeeding is magnificent, it entails pain, discomfort, and dissatisfaction. As such, do not glamorize struggling, but rather the goal, success, pleasure, or enlightenment at the end of the struggle.

Hyper-focusing on the negative aspects of life is another trigger of negative thought processes. Things like terror, warfare, and violence are all around us, and they are the obsession of news giants. Some social media platforms also fixate on negative posts. However, good things must be considered, such as a child getting their qualification or a woman starting her own business. Focusing on the good and the bad gives you a more balanced perspective.

Likewise, we naturally resort to negative thinking when faced with difficult situations. However, certain personal experiences can further worsen this tendency. For instance, discovering that you have a medical condition beyond your control can be a major blow to your mental well-being. Similarly, dealing with persistent mental health issues can also be taxing. Yet, cultivating an optimistic mindset is crucial to achieving a fulfilling and satisfying life. Even if nothing good is happening, focusing on the small things that bring you joy or comfort can make a difference. With a concerted effort to shift your thinking, you can empower yourself to take on life's challenges with a renewed sense of purpose and resilience.

Another thing that is less under our direct control is the genetic and evolutionary necessity to fight for survival. This need is hardwired into our existence and can cause us to see threats from multiple directions, even when no real threats are present. The fight or flight mechanism can also activate this need for survival. When the fight or flight mechanism is activated, you tend to feel a more vital need to protect yourself and the things you love. This mechanism might result in you *"protecting"* against people and conditions that posed no harm or negativity to you in the first place.

Hence, negative thinking patterns can have various causes, some discussed above. However, there may be other triggers that lead to negative thoughts. The key to overcoming these patterns is to identify the root cause. This involves actively searching for the trigger, labeling it, and taking control of the situation. By knowing what you are dealing with, you can take the first step towards overcoming negative thought patterns and leading a more positive life.

Cognitive Distortion

Cognitive distortions, to be precise, are alterations of the truth by someone's mind. A less common variation of this is altering things into positives when they are anything but positive. Meanwhile, the distortion of reality into a negative leads to self-destructive conduct and long-term unhappiness, which differs from an adverse take on reality based on singular observations or incidents.

On a deeper level, cognitive distortions result in nihilistic thinking. Nihilism denies the possibility of truth and objective reality. Instead, it purports that life is meaningless and that there is no point in anything. When someone prescribes this philosophy, they often state that there is no such thing as morals, values, or ethics because life is innate and without meaning. This type of thinking can lead you into distortions that suck out the joy and pleasure from life. It also makes it difficult to see any good or fun in yourself or the people around you, which puts you in a low emotional state.

Common causes of distortion are overthinking, cynical hostility, and rumination. Overthinking is when you keep thinking about something to get *"every possible angle"* on an issue. When things do not align with one of those plans or predictions, it induces cognitive distortions that either explain away the failure or hold you accountable for it. The result is changing your observations of reality from the cold facts, which makes you less able to deal with your daily demands.

Meanwhile, cynical hostility is when you believe something wrong about another person, and you overtly communicate this. Likely, you consider them useless, nasty, or fake people, amongst other things. A cynical view can lead to a reluctance to depend on others as a source of support. Likewise, it makes you unable to maintain healthy relationships where you can receive emotional support and process life experiences. The outcome of this can lead to unhelpful and unhealthy distortions about both yourself and other people. Practice empathy exercises as one of the first steps towards preventing this cause of cognitive distortion. As such, take a few moments to close your eyes and imagine yourself in someone else's shoes. Imagine what it would feel like to be that person and experience the situation they are going through. Allow yourself to feel their emotions and try to understand their perspective without judgment. You can also ask yourself questions like: *"What might be causing them to act this way?"* or *"What struggles might they be going through that I do not know about?"*

Then, rumination is when you think about your flaws or the things you have not done well. You fixate on the negative things linked to you, making it challenging to feel proactive about doing better in the future. Going over and over bad things that have happened in your head will cause you to start using cognitive distortions that break down your good qualities more. Doing something to occupy your mind with more positive things stops this process. Occupation of your mind by positive things is done by participating in pleasant activities, doing hobbies, reading, and doing things around the house that keep you out of your mind.

One of the most common cognitive distortions is blaming others for your problems or blaming yourself for all the bad things that have happened. Another is believing you are not worthy of love, success, or good things. Likewise, being guilty of something you have no control over. The distortion that everyone hates you or lies to you takes this to the extreme. Trying to find every possible point to destroy yourself or your well-being is another common distortion, as well as believing that someone else's problems or stresses are so crucial that yours do not matter. Hence, the list of possible distortions is endless.

Observing when you use distortions is the first step to overcoming them. Noticing incongruity between facts and thoughts is a way to recognize distortions. Breaking yourself down when you are progressing is one such case, like a bodybuilder criticizing themselves when their size, weight, and endurance have increased. Listen to how you phrase things in your internal dialogue, particularly negatively-worded statements. For instance, when you struggle with your studies and start thinking with pessimistic ideas, you can alter them to *"I am taking steps to improve my academic results."* This statement validates the steps you are taking.

Spotting generalizations in your thoughts is also an excellent way to notice distortions. When you are generalizing single incidents into descriptions of your whole life or personality, review what you say and rephrase it to what is happening. Changing *"I am stupid"* to *"I did not do well on that test"* is more precise and less self-destructive. Looking for the word *"should"* is another way of spotting distortions. It can be a demotivating word that shows us what we are not doing or have not achieved yet.

Likewise, making assumptions about people or situations is a distortion sneaking up in your mind. It makes you feel as if people see you in a bad light or that you should see others in such a light. Before jumping to conclusions, ask those involved about the matter. As such, they can describe what is going on or what they are thinking without needing you to figure it out with assumptions. Make an investigation into a subject if you must determine the facts. Investigating is also a good course of action when you have already come to conclusions based purely on opinion and want to *"confirm"* the view. Such clarification changes *"having to be right"* to being right or correcting any findings that might be wrong.

The point is not to run away from the negatives in our minds but to change them so that we feel empowered about the change we are already making. Suppose you are motivated to do something about it. In that case, you are far more likely to move past distortions in place and face situations as they are. Living a life without filters is ideal. You accomplish unfiltered thinking when you face things as they are and are willing to tackle challenges. When you see things as they are, you may also notice that a lot of the *"negative"* that you are taking on has nothing to do with you in the first place. They are someone else's problem. Even if you can contribute by helping them, it would not allow you or those you can positively impact if you hyperfocus on one person who is draining your emotional and mental resources.

The point of the matter is to make progress. There might be many changes before the adverse scenario is entirely out of the way, but taking the next step towards that allows you to focus without overwhelming yourself with the entire problem.

Types of Negative Thinking Patterns

There are many common types of thinking patterns with adverse effects. Some of the most common types are categorized and described here.

Jumping to conclusions is when you interpret and label something, usually about yourself, negatively, without examining the situation to determine the facts. The result is that you have a *"decisive"* opinion about a quality that is bad or something negative. Non-factual, permanent, negative sentiments result from the inability and unwillingness to change views. When this happens, the way to break the habit is first to examine the critical things you jump to conclusions about before giving them a label.

Jumping to conclusions is similar to the negative thinking pattern of overgeneralizing, wherein you make one incident into an overarching description—blowing a car accident into the idea that you are the worst driver to exist and that your license should get revoked is one such case. A related pattern is to filter out the good and only validate the bad mentally. You may look at the times you made mistakes while doing something and make it out as if you only ever make mistakes. Yet, you may be a person that often achieves well in your consideration, but you are ignoring the good you have done.

Another pattern is labeling or mislabeling. This is taking a situation, incident, or characteristic and making it very broad—an incident such as the case of a child dropping a glass. After generalizing, you give it a label, but the designation is often of an inflammatory or extreme nature. The child who dropped the glass could be told, *"You are a klutz,"* or some similar label. The child is then broken down to some degree on an emotional or psychological level and may, in turn, become a clumsy and foolish person to fit the mold that is repeated to them.

Fortune telling is a pattern in which you assume something about the future (something undesirable) and resign yourself to it happening. There is no effort to change what you believe may occur, thus making it more likely to come into being. Almost the opposite of this, but not entirely, is placing imperatives on yourself. By telling yourself how things *"should"* or *"must"* be, you do everything you can to alter existing conditions or the progress of things so that they mirror the imperative statement. Although it might give you a sense of motivation on some level, the problem with this is that it puts you into overdrive and causes burnout. Moreover, you will feel guilty or inadequate if you do not fulfill the imperative, leading to self-degrading opinions.

Self-blame is a process in which you personalize bad things around you. In other words, you blame yourself for adverse conditions, even though you do not cause them. Unpleasant personalization could be the case when a loved one gets injured or diagnosed with a terminal illness—you blame yourself even though you could not possibly have been the cause. Fairness fallacies are a different negative thinking pattern that you might get in similar circumstances. This type of thinking relates to believing the world is unfair and that others are to blame for how complicated life is. Even though those people were not the reason you or someone close to you is going through an experience, you still feel like they are to blame or that the world's unfairness is somehow attributable to them. In the case of an ill family member, this could manifest by blaming another successful family member for the condition because they cannot *"save"* the sick person.

Change is another condition that is prone to producing fallacies. In this mental process, you project your desires onto someone. You expect them to mold to your needs or wants, placing unfair expectations on them. Emotional reasoning is a process that might have similar results in how you treat a person. In this case, your feelings tell you what a person must be like or have done, not objective facts or what they have to say for themselves. They cannot influence your opinion because your emotions have already resulted in an ironclad conclusion about them. As a result, they will either try very hard to change so that you improve your opinion of them, or they will move on and leave you without their presence.

Likewise, polarization is another process that might result in you having an overly harsh opinion of someone. You see things in two categories, either right or wrong, with no room in the middle. Thus, someone is either wholly problematic or undesirable, or they are a miracle worker or worthy of complete admiration. Polarization can lead to simplifying life into a competitive mentality in which you are against people that fall into the lower two categories and might even lead you to justify malicious conduct against them. The inability to be wrong is a thought process that can have the same result on your behavior towards another. You must be right with such a necessity that even the bad things you do to others have a *"logical"* explanation. There is no room for admitting mistakes, which means there is no room for you to grow in your conduct.

When you *"read someone's mind"* and determine what they think about you, this mental process is going to result in a negative impact on the relationships you have. You conclude what they think of you or some subject based on your opinion (or by taking one statement as their underlying opinion). Deducing like this is similar to using emotional reasoning. Not only might they take this as offensive, but there may be far more to their thoughts and opinions about you or the subject, as people are more complex than single statements they make.

We've all seen arguments evolve for exactly this reason. An example is a friend who opens up about something sensitive, such as wanting to adopt a baby. The friend she's talking to asks her if she's thought through all the responsibilities. Affront gets taken as she feels like the friend says she's not responsible enough. While this was likely not the intention, a rift develops, and the relationship between the friends ends.

A duo of thought processes is opposites, yet both will negatively affect your life. Magnification is on the one end of the spectrum. In this case, you take your mistakes (even minute ones) and make it seem like you caused the catastrophe. On the other end, there is minimizing, in which you look at the positive things you have done and pretend they do not exist. The hyperfocus of the first thought process is the things you do wrong, while the second process purposefully discounts and places no focus on the good.

A final typical negative thought process that is worth mentioning is the control fallacy. This fallacy has two main versions. First, you believe you control every terrible thing in your life, blame yourself, and induce self-guilt. While the second version is where you think you have no control over your life. You feel like the good and bad things happen without any influence from you, resulting in you feeling powerless. Both result in thought processes that make life unnecessarily difficult.

You can use healthy activities to break out negative thought patterns. They include meditation, keeping a journal, exercising, yoga, and breathing exercises. Changing your mindset by dedicating time each day to finding things to love about yourself, seeing beauty in the world, replacing evil thoughts with better ones, and being honest with yourself will contribute to breaking out of negative habits. The way you plan out your time also plays a big part. Suppose you schedule a time to think negatively. In that case, you can put negative thoughts on hold to look at during that time (often because you forget about the negative review altogether). Reducing your time on social media and news sites will also be a healthy way to spend your time better to overcome negative thoughts.

Chapter 4:
Controlling Thoughts and Emotions

The powerful forces of our thoughts and emotions greatly influence our daily lives. They can inspire us toward greatness, hold us back, and cause undue stress and anxiety. However, imagine controlling these inner workings instead of being controlled by them. While it may be challenging, taking charge of our emotions and thoughts with such techniques.

Focus

In today's fast-paced world, distractions are ubiquitous. As such, our attention is constantly being pulled in multiple directions. Likely from the constant buzz of notifications or the temptation of watching viral videos. As a result, our attention spans are shrinking, and our ability to concentrate diminishes. However, our focus can be strengthened through regular practice and a change in habits.

Studies have shown that overstimulation is the root cause of distraction. The constant barrage of information we receive through our devices triggers the release of dopamine, a neurotransmitter that produces pleasure. This dopamine rush entices us to seek more stimulation. Hence, leading to a vicious cycle of addiction and the need for constant mental stimulation. To combat this, we need to give our brains a break from external stimulation through regular periods of boredom.

For instance, set aside time to unplug your devices. Alternatively, engage in activities that require minimal mental stimulation, like gardening or cleaning. This way, you allow our minds to rest and refocus. Likewise, we can process our thoughts and emotions during this time without external distractions. Thus, not only it strengthens our attention span, but it also promotes creativity and self-awareness.

But what happens when these boredom breaks are not enough? When our ability to focus is impeded by overstimulation, it may be time for a stimulus cleanse. For example, a technology cleanse of at least eight days can help restore attention spans and make focusing easier. During this time, we should abstain from all technological input, such as social media, emails, and phone calls. Then, engage in enriching yet low-stimulus activities such as reading, hiking, or drawing. By breaking free from our addiction to external stimuli, we allow ourselves to recalibrate and reset our minds. Once we do this, focusing becomes more natural, and distractions become easier to ignore.

Hence, improving our focus takes time and effort, but the benefits are extensive. By incorporating regular boredom breaks and stimulus cleanses, we can train our minds to use focus more effectively. Besides that, we can tune out distractions, complete our work more efficiently, and achieve our goals with more clarity and less stress.

The 5 Pillars of Mental Performance

Positive Thinking

Positive thinking is crucial in our lives, especially during difficult times. It helps uplift our spirits, providing us the drive to succeed and progress. While it is not always possible to think positively all the time, there are ways to train our minds to focus on the positive.

Usually, demotivation or lack of confidence hit us. Yet, examining these thoughts can uncover which areas of your mind require change. Take a moment to slow down and assess whether your thoughts are mostly positive or negative. For instance, if you have negative thoughts in certain areas, such as your career, relationships, or personal growth, it is time to rephrase them with positive affirmations.

Regularly reviewing your thoughts is a valuable exercise that can help you develop a more positive mindset. Not only can it help you identify problematic areas of your mind, but it can also reveal which parts of your life need the most attention. By listing positive affirmations related to these areas and rephrasing your thoughts, you can change your thinking patterns and become more optimistic.

Consequently, this exercise helps you break ingrained thought patterns that hold you back. Likewise, by taking regular *"pit stops"* throughout the day to examine your thoughts, you can form lasting habits that promote positivity and personal growth. With time and practice, positive thinking will become a natural part of your mindset.

Adding humor into your daily routine could also greatly benefit your overall mood and wellness. Not only does laughter increase happiness, but it also helps to reduce stress and tension that may have built up. However, try thinking outside the box and incorporating humor into social settings instead of settling for easy laughs from funny videos or shows. As such, attending comedy readings or live shows from famous comedians not only provides a good laugh. Yet, it also offers opportunities for camaraderie and potential friendship.

Another way to utilize humor is by directing it towards negative thoughts and phrases that often repeat in our minds. By exaggerating these phrases with an overly dramatic or odd-sounding voice, we can decrease their negative impact on our mood. Let us say you have a negative thought that keeps repeating, such as *"I am not good enough."* Whenever this thought comes up, you can exaggerate it with a silly voice and make it sound absurd. For example, you could say, *"Oh no, I am not good enough! I might as well crawl under a rock and never return!"* The ridiculousness of this exercise can help snap us out of a foul mood. Likewise, it reframes our thoughts towards a more positive and humorous perspective.

Moreover, surrounding ourselves with people who inspire, support, and brighten our day brings positivity. Meanwhile, constantly being around negative individuals can harm our mental health. While removing completely negative people from our lives may not be possible, we can distance ourselves from them. Alternatively, focus more on the positive people in our life. These individuals uplift us and bring us to a brighter outlook on life. Their presence enhances the possibility of achieving our goals, passions, and dreams. Studies show that positive, supportive social environments have significant psychological benefits. Such benefits include releasing oxytocin, which promotes feelings of happiness and belonging.

Aside from that, incorporate positive self-talk into your life while altering your thinking patterns. Talk or think to yourself kindly and treat yourself like a friend or someone you like. Find the good qualities within yourself and acknowledge them. As media personality RuPaul says, *"If you cannot love yourself, how will you love somebody else?"* Or, phrased for our purposes, you must start by loving yourself and appreciating the good within you. Finding things about yourself that you are grateful for is a great starting point for instigating positive self-talk habits.

Positive affirmations are an effective tool for improving the positivity of your thinking. They ingrain the habit of thinking positively using repetition. But there are a few things you can do to make the affirmations even more effective. The first is to tailor the affirmations to your life, personalizing them. Stating affirmations in language that is non-generalized will be more impactful and *"real"* to you. Phrase the affirmation in the present, repeat it regularly, and you are bound to influence your subconscious and unconscious thoughts faster.

Likewise, healthy physical habits make for a massive boost in positivity. When sleepy, you can hardly focus on achieving and feeling good about the world. The same goes for feeling too hungry or too full throughout the day. Taking care of your body brings back a sense of personal confidence. It also lets your mind and body cooperate better and work more like a smooth whirring machine. A higher level of comfort, health, and self-assurance will strongly impact the positivity of your thoughts and emotions—along with the boost you might get from compliments others give you.

A final step for positive thinking is to act on your decisions or what you tell yourself. Carrying your thoughts into the physical world will allow you to achieve outcomes. Obtaining results raises confidence in yourself, which cements the power of your positive reviews. And suppose the actions do not bring about the results you intended. In that case, you can learn and alter your thinking towards a different approach to the situation.

Visualization

Visualization is an exercise to imagine different scenarios, whether for problem-solving, relaxation, or manifestation.

When doing visualization to manifest, the first step is to know what you want. In the case of using it to display better thought and emotion control, you want smooth self-control. Having this in mind gives you something to work towards and to picture as your end goal. Mindfulness meditation lets you envision your desired objective, such as imagining the physical sensations you will feel while remaining in control in challenging situations.

The visualization should have much detail to it. The details of the surroundings, including all the senses you can imagine in the situation. Picture the things you will see around you, the smells of the people and vicinity, or the sounds in the background. Picturing the internal details will take it that much further as an experience, such as imagining your temperature, the sensations within your body, the position you will be in, and any aches or physical comforts.

Subsequently, incorporate emotions to picture yourself handling them expertly. Imagine the feelings you receive from others. You can even color the feelings in the visualization to add nuance to the experience. Picture remaining uninfluenced by the emotions or reacting appropriately to the scenario. Likewise, you can even picture how the color of the emotion you received alters when you process it into a more pleasant color, thus showing yourself exuding a positive influence in the situation. In visualizing the feelings, you may feel them, which is okay. Just acknowledge and accept the emotions, as all emotions are part of the spectrum of what you may think in the future. The trick is to see how you will handle those emotions, using them as an impetus for the progression of your goals.

Daily visualization will make it a habit to expertly handle your thoughts and emotions. Eventually, you would not just be imagining the flows and reactions of thoughts and feelings. Still, you will be practicing what you pictured. Not too long into the future, it will become second nature to visualize how you will overcome complicated situations, making it gradually easier to face challenges composed and confidently.

A final piece of advice is to have the fortitude necessary to keep going with your visualization, even in situations that are not easy to face. Remember that while it might be uncomfortable to imagine the issue, it is still more pleasant than going through it. By facing it now in your mind's eye, you will make it easier to meet later.

Guided Imagery

Guided imagery is similar to visualization in that you picture something in your mind. Use it to instill the idea of a calm environment so that your mind and body both relax. The fight or flight response gets activated throughout the day in the modern world, even when there is no call for it. Overstimulation is partly the cause of this, both in terms of entertainment and the work you complete. Using guided imagery relaxes the response and lets you take on a focused mindset once again.

First, find a comfortable place to do the guided imagery session. The location should preferably be somewhere away from people. As such, people staring in at you or trying to ask you questions is distracting and defeats the purpose of calming down. You may also want a comfortable seat to take full advantage of the imagery. Sitting in an uncomfortable position or on something that does not feel right might make it difficult to immerse yourself in the full benefits.

Guided imagery audio will also be necessary. The best is a life instructor of the course. In most cases, this would not be accessible. Use resources such as YouTube or guided meditation apps such as Headspace that will provide you with audio to follow. Alternatively, you could read through a few scripts and follow their instructions as you go along. Using a script is not ideal because you will have to open your eyes constantly to look at the next step, or you will have to memorize a whole list of instructions.

Having headphones could also be beneficial, especially if they are noise-canceling ones. The imagery is more easily accessible when you cancel out the surrounding world. There will be less room for distraction, and people tend to bother you less when you wear headphones. They assume you are listening to music or are on a call and are not available to speak (most people, at least). Further, with guided meditation on apps and YouTube, there is often calming music playing in the background that can enhance the quality of the experience.

The purpose of guided imagery is to reduce stress levels. With reduced stress levels, keeping your mind under control and your thoughts on track toward your goals or tasks will be easier. Your emotions will also come through with less intensity, making it easier to feel focused.

Meditation

An ancient technique that many cultures have used throughout history, meditation, is known as a practice that can bring an innate sense of calm into people. You can use meditation regularly over your whole life for a calmer and more positive outlook on life in general. Similarly, you can use it to overcome or subdue spikes of emotional overwhelm. Consistent meditation can help build resilience and prepare us to face challenges head-on. In particular, mindfulness meditation can bring you to the present, allowing you to stay focused on the task.

Despite that, many people struggle with meditation because they believe they must empty their minds of all thoughts. Yet, this is far from the truth. While some forms of meditation suggest focusing solely on breathing or a single image, for most of us, having thoughts during meditation is natural. In fact, thoughts can be considered an integral part of meditation.

As such, acknowledge the thoughts without dwelling on them. Then, if you are doing a meditative technique that calls for attention to your breathing, gently bring your attention to your breath. Meanwhile, if the meditation calls for something else, like feeling the pressure of the floor, being aware of the environment, or visualizing something, then bring your attention to the session's object. The thing to know is that there are many thoughts in our minds constantly, so some will naturally come up in your mind during the session. Accept them, do not obsess over blocking them out, then bring your focus back to what you are doing—it is as simple as that.

Like guided imagery and other relaxation exercises, doing it daily (or at least regularly) produces the most benefits. While meditation will calm you down when you use it during a particularly rough time, it will have much stronger effects when compounded by daily sessions. Taking a few minutes each day to do this is calming and allows you to manage stress better overall. Your emotions do not spike as often, and you will find you are much more in control of your mind and attention.

The perceptions you use while doing meditation should not only be limited to the inner feeling of your body and the touch of the floor. A multi-dimensional experience will elevate the quality of your meditation. Sense the smells with your nose, the temperature of the air, the loudness or quietness of the environment, the light coming through your eyelids, the taste in your mouth, and so much more. You will find that, by doing this, you also improve the quality of your lived experiences outside of your meditation sessions. Not to mention, you will find it easier to control your senses, thus making it easier to focus your attention.

The main requirements with meditation are a comfortable and quiet space and somewhere comfortable to sit. You can add other touches, such as guided meditation audio (different from guided imagery) or music. An aromatherapy diffuser can also be a pleasant touch, but all you need is a space where you will be calmly uninterrupted for your session, so something like a car seat or park bench will work quite well too.

There are many meditation methods that you could use. Some of them are mindfulness meditation and body scanning meditation. Mindfulness meditation is one of the most effective for pulling out the storms of thoughts in your mind because the focus is on bringing your attention to the present. Meanwhile, body scanning meditation can help you calm the body down and to bring your attention away from your thoughts and emotions. Instead of trying to stop thoughts and feelings, you are directing your attention somewhere specific, like what you would experience during progressive muscle relaxation. Other beneficial meditation practices for better control of your thoughts and emotions include breathing meditation, meditating with a mantra, or using positive affirmations.

Pillar 3:
Emotional Agility

Emotional agility is a relatively new topic, but it is one of the most empowering approaches to your mental health that you can follow. The next three chapters will explore what it is, how it works, and what you can get from it.

Chapter 5:
Learning Emotional Agility

Emotional agility is an empowering practice that involves embracing our emotions without reservation. Through introspection and self-mastery, we can unleash our inner potential and grow into the best versions of ourselves. When we accept our feelings as valid and acknowledge them for what they are, we create space for growth and development.

Embracing emotional agility allows us to respond appropriately to circumstances. Likewise, it aligns our emotions with our intentions and actions. As such, it makes our emotions more fluid and adaptable, allowing us to use them as an impetus to achieve our goals. These consequences are significant in our fast-paced world, where change is the only constant.

What is Emotional Agility?

Being aware of our emotions and acknowledging and accepting them without judgment is emotional agility. Developing emotional agility requires a rich emotional vocabulary beyond a few basic emotions. In essence, it means identifying and naming a wide range of emotions. There are nuances to every emotion, and accurately labeling them leads to a deeper understanding of yourself. For instance, there is a difference between being anxious and being ruffled. With the latter, it implies that you were initially calm, but something has now caused you to feel uneasy. Being ruffled shows, there is something you disagree with or were surprised about, resulting in a feeling of unease.

Incorporating labels into your emotions can give you a better understanding of them. Plus, it creates some distance between yourself and the feeling. For instance, feeling upset or agitated can be labeled as *"ruffled"* to help you realize that something has disrupted your sense of calmness. This heightened awareness allows you to examine the source of your discomfort. Then, address any bottled emotions or memories that need attention. Through this process, our brains can process emotions more effectively. Thus, allowing us to regulate better and manage our moods.

After placing a gap between yourself and the emotions you are experiencing, you will have the chance to let go of them. Your perspective expands from the single incident and allows you to look at the bigger picture. Observing their origins allows you to work through any causes of fixations or stuck emotions. As a result, you gain greater flexibility and resilience in managing your emotional well-being. Rather than fixating on the incident that triggered the emotion, you can move beyond it and avoid getting trapped in a one-track experience.

To practice emotional agility, here are some steps you could follow:

1. **Recognize and label your emotions.** Take a moment to identify what you are feeling and give it a name. Try to be specific and use descriptive words that accurately describe the intensity and nature of your emotions.

2. **Accept and appreciate your emotions.** Rather than suppressing or denying your emotions, acknowledge them. Recognize that all feelings are natural human experiences.

3. **Detach from your emotions.** Step back from your emotions and observe them as an outside observer. Avoid getting caught up in the intensity of your emotions and instead try to remain objective.

4. **Reframe your emotions.** Instead of viewing your emotions as positive or negative, reframe them as helpful or unhelpful. Ask yourself what purpose your emotions serve and how they can be useful.

5. **Take action.** Once you better understand your emotions and their purpose, constructively respond to them. This may involve changing your behavior, seeking support from others, or engaging in self-care activities.

Furthermore, properly letting go of the emotion related to the experience will require understanding your *'why.'* This *'why'* is something that gives you drive in life. It is more than just some passion or targets, but a more profound driving power. When you know what drives you, you can move beyond the imperatives and focus on where you want to get to in life. While you may meet basic survival needs, the desire for more will drive you to work harder and more passionately to achieve your goals. Understanding your purpose also allows you to make sense of your emotions and see how they align or diverge with various experiences.

Seeing the link between your *'why'* and your emotions will create a clearer path for your future actions. Subsequently, it lets you see how your behavior can contribute to your goals. Thus, you would not feel as disconnected from your emotional responses because you know the underlying reasons for their emergence. As such, instead of being impulsive and momentary, they become part of a broader, more enduring pattern.

Likewise, your *'why'* will give you a better glimpse into your values. These values are constantly present and help align your actions with your identity. Knowing them shows what is important to you, which you need to know when working out the morals and behaviors you want to embody daily. Having core values guides your actions, even in situations you have never experienced. As a result, you will be flexible and capable of thinking on your feet.

Once your values are clear to you, you must gather enough courage to live by them. The environment around you, including your family, culture, and nation, will dictate to you what is important to them. If you build up the fortitude you need, you can exert your values amongst all this. Understanding yourself better by building emotional agility relies on understanding your own beliefs.

Understanding Emotions

When it comes to your emotions, they can be difficult to pinpoint and describe accurately. Often, they can feel amorphous and difficult to put into words. However, emotions are very much real, both on a mental and physical level. To better understand your emotional experiences, expand your emotional vocabulary. By doing so, you can more effectively interpret your emotional responses to any given situation. This process becomes easier with time as you see patterns and similarities in your emotional experiences.

Meanwhile, sometimes we tempt to present a façade to the world in such situations. However, these unprocessed emotions can build up and become a tangled mess of unresolved feelings. Subsequently, this accumulation of emotions can lead to mental health problems. Or worst, it may turn to unhealthy coping mechanisms such as substance abuse or overeating to manage.

For instance, imagine someone consistently suppresses their anger and never addresses the underlying issues causing it. Likely, they may feel a sense of frustration, resentment, or bitterness toward themselves and others. Then, these feelings can lead to a buildup of negative emotions, causing them to experience symptoms of anxiety and depression. In this way, unprocessed emotions can manifest as mental health issues.

Working through an emotional experience may be uncomfortable and unpleasant. Still, it is necessary to achieve closure and move forward with a clearer understanding of how to navigate future challenges. Avoiding emotions only leads to further emotional baggage and mental health issues. Yet, confronting them head-on can promote emotional growth and flexibility. Moreover, emotions are a powerful and complex aspect of the human experience. At times, they can lift us to heights we never thought possible, while at other times, they can crush us down into despair. No matter how intense or fleeting they may seem, all emotions have the potential to influence our lives in significant ways. But with emotional agility, we can navigate these emotional highs and lows and maintain our focus on their goals.

If you need more perspective on the situation, contact someone you trust, such as a friend, family member, therapist, or colleague. The important thing is that it should be someone who will listen to what you have to say without judgment. Sometimes, voicing your emotions is all you need because it allows you to determine what is happening and what to do about it. Other times, you might find opinions from the other person helpful. Their points of view come from different perspectives from yours. They, thus, might provide insight that you would never have considered otherwise.

Besides that, avoid thinking of emotions as either positive or negative since it is not always the case. Sometimes emotions are a mixture of both. Being stuck in one emotional state can be problematic since it can make life more difficult. Additionally, when it comes to experiencing emotions, it is necessary to recognize that different situations call for different emotional responses. In such situations, our emotional intelligence help regulate our emotional states and respond appropriately.

For example, grieving the loss of a loved one is appropriate and healthy. Feeling the emotion will lead to processing the situation better. When you accept the grief that comes with the loss, you can let it out and come to grips with that person no longer being with you. That said, if you try to act as if everything is fine, you set yourself up for fake emotions and *"pretty"* facades. Yet, the situation would be different if someone who passed was horrible and continually shut down your creativity and ambition. In this case, you may feel relief and sense the pressure shifting off your shoulders.

Additionally, positive and negative emotions can serve as a driving force to push us toward our goals. As such, although perceived as a negative emotion, anger can be a powerful driver for change. Suppose you are driven by providing justice to your community. By highlighting unacceptable conditions and injustices, anger can help draw the community's attention and rally them behind your cause. This, in turn, can increase public support and push decision-makers to adopt policies and measures that promote fairness and equality.

Thus, what we choose to do with our emotions is one of the most important parts of experiencing them. When we observe and accept them, we can manage them in the direction we need to achieve our life goals. Looking at your emotions directly and objectively will allow you to use them to bring positive change. However, avoiding them can lead you down a path of destruction and hinder your chances of survival. The following two sections take a more detailed review of emotions we traditionally consider positive and negative.

Positive

Positive emotions are those we seek out, such as joy, triumph, exhilaration, curiosity, excitement, and love. Investing in these positive emotions lets us grow and become better individuals. Emotions like excitement and love drive us forward, helping us to develop new skills and experiences that offer a sense of achievement. Furthermore, these positive emotional experiences give us a sense of healthiness and contentment, which is essential for overall well-being.

However, in life, people use the promise of pleasurable emotions to get others to do things with the aim of manipulation. Suppose a salesperson persuades a potential customer to buy an expensive product by promising they will experience a sense of luxury and exclusivity. The salesperson may use tactics such as emphasizing the high status of the product, highlighting the potential admiration and envy of others, or offering special perks or discounts to sweeten the deal. In doing so, the customer may be manipulated into purchasing based on the promise of experiencing pleasurable emotions associated with the product and the status it confers, even if they do not truly need or want the item.

Although pleasurable emotions can be desirable, they can also bring stress into our life. Pursuing a goal and striving for a desirable feeling often involves facing challenges and difficulties. However, the promise of achieving the desired outcome and the correlated pleasant emotion can instill resilience and determination. As such, desire can be a stronger motivator than fear of pain or failure, especially for a feeling we perceive as positive. As a result, we may be willing to exert more effort and endure more stress to attain that positive emotion.

Thus, positive emotions can be good and bad, depending on how they are experienced and used. When you use them as a source for manipulation, they are negative; but if you use them to instill a passion for attainment, their impact can be beyond positive.

Negative

Negative emotions are commonly avoided and considered unpleasant experiences. These emotions can be challenging and drive us to seek immediate relief. However, negative emotions can also catalyze to push us toward positive change. When utilized correctly, negative emotions can motivate us to work through them quickly.

Nevertheless, if ignored or suppressed, negative emotions can lead to mental health conditions that make it difficult to escape an endless cycle of negativity. To avoid this, we must confront our negative emotions and work through them. The approach may vary, depending on the situation and the individual's emotional disposition. Sometimes, a firm and direct approach is necessary. At other times, a gentler and more gradual approach may work better. The negative emotion's intensity and duration should determine the approach taken.

Other effects of ignoring negative emotions for a long time are dysfunctional attitudes. These types of attitudes are when you feel depressed. Feeling down results in seeing yourself, the future, or other people in an unpleasant guise. When it negatively affects your outlook on things to come, the attitude is striking at your goals and reasons to live. To avoid this, some people resort to unrealistic ideas, such as flights of fancy or delusions.

Delusions or distortions of reality are a breeding ground for more negative emotions. They result from inaccurate observations of the world around you. As such, a feeling of misunderstanding will always lurk in the background. Delusions cause underlying feelings to fester away underneath. To face the underlying emotion is the crux of getting rid of the delusions and seeing the world as it is again. Learning coping mechanisms will help you handle negative emotions in the long run.

The **ABC Model** is a helpful explanation of how things unfold with negative emotions that are left unchecked. First, there is *'A' (an activating event)*, which is going through an experience you did not like. Then, *'B' (a belief)* is an opinion you hold that is not empowering and not quite right, such as seeing yourself as weak for not coping with the stress of the activating event. Then, *'C' (the consequence)* is the emotion you feel due to the negative belief, which could be disappointment, sadness, or anger in this example. One of the best coping mechanisms to overcome the ABC mechanism is looking at the belief you developed after the activating event and breaking it down with your power of observation. The result is that the consequent emotion will reduce in intensity and any reality distortion will ease.

Thus, not all emotions are negative or positive. Some fall right in the middle as neutral emotions. These emotions are the ones we tend to feel almost daily. They include boredom, indifference, mild interest, and resignation. Whatever the sentiment, whether positive, negative, or neutral, the value of it lies in how you use the emotion to get yourself in action toward your goals. A positive feeling can be a powerful motivator, propelling you to pursue your goals. At the same time, negative emotion can function as a warning not to veer too far from the path of your values. Finally, neutral feelings form the easy foundation upon which you can rest while focusing on getting things done.

Now that we have broken down emotions as a topic, we will explain how to build emotional agility.

Chapter 6:
How to Build Emotional Agility

Building emotional agility involves developing the ability to navigate various emotions and adapt to changing circumstances. Yet, emotional agility is not only essential for personal growth. In fact, it also improves relationships and overall well-being. Likewise, it involves using our emotions to make intentional and constructive choices. By doing so, we can overcome obstacles, make better decisions, and lead a more fulfilling life.

Managing Your Emotions

Have you ever had someone misunderstand the emotions you were trying to convey? Maybe you were anxious about a situation, but you came across as angry instead of showing anxiety. Unfortunately, this misinterpretation can lead to misunderstandings and even tensions with those around you. Yet, this is just one example of how emotions can directly impact our lives. Emotions can pack a punch with varying intensities, whether positive, negative, or neutral. That said, managing your emotions before they spiral out of control is necessary. After all, the outcomes of your feelings can be far-reaching, affecting not only your personal life but also your professional success.

The first step towards managing your emotions is *not to squash them down unnecessarily*. Suppressing them leads to unhealthy conditions such as depression and mania. Facing your emotions is how to prevent them from bottling up, which might require you to learn some coping techniques. Suppose emotions are intense or challenging to meet. In that case, a coping strategy can help you stand up to the weight of the feeling and process it, even if it is only a bit at a time. Doing this will reduce emotional outbursts because you will be working through them regularly, removing the necessity for them to rush out in one fell swoop.

Accept your emotions by approving of their validity. This simple act is a powerful way of cultivating self-trust and improving your emotional well-being. Understanding and accepting your emotions gives you clarity and insight into how they fit into your reactions and life goals. Although expressing your emotions in all situations is not always suitable, accepting them gives you the confidence to express them appropriately at the right time and place. For example, if you are about to conduct an important presentation, you will want to put on a professional front and keep your emotions in check. Nonetheless, accepting your emotions and their validity allows you to process them, work out their logical cause, and deal with them adequately later.

Working out the cause of an emotion is also a valid coping mechanism. The situation that gave rise to the feeling had some interaction with your values and why. It is good to see where the link lies because then the logic of it all fits together. Another factor to consider is what you can do to align your values with the actions you want to do on impulse because of the emotions. In this way, you can channel your feelings in a direction that will advance your goals.

For example, when you are confused about a newly-installed system at work and your goal is to become the trainer for new employees in the long run, direct the emotion of confusion to your HR department. Work out a teaching program to ensure future employees understand the system. The HR individual will be able to connect with you about the emotion of confusion, and they will see that you are passionate about making the system more understandable for others. Presenting a teaching plan shows you are serious about your topic. When a trainer position opens, their experience with you will come to mind. They will consider you a strong candidate, knowing you are passionate about teaching roles.

Mindfulness

Mindfulness is a transformative state of attention where we actively focus on our present being. By mindfully experiencing the present, we gain greater clarity and focus on the world around us without the interference of our thoughts and preoccupations. This level of awareness fosters a sense of inner calm and stability, even in the face of stress and pressure. In fact, those who frequently engage with mindfulness techniques are often more resilient to life's challenges, as they maintain composure and clarity of purpose in times of difficulty.

There are exercises you can do to improve your capacity to use mindfulness. Opening neural pathways allow you to operate more in the present. Older neural pathways that enable unfiltered emotions to fly in and out are gradually eased into inactivity, making it easier for you to be naturally focused. You then become resilient to stress by reacting with focus on the tasks in front of you as a habit, which results in assignments getting completed and handling the cause of the pressure.

Deep breathing and breathwork are ways in which you can practice mindfulness. Your breath is a constant. As such, you can always bring your attention to it in the present, whether fast or slow. The first step is focusing on it and observing your breathing without trying to change it. Once your attention is there and you have observed how you are breathing, you can start taking deeper breaths.

Taking deeper breaths allows more oxygen to enter your body and reduces your fight or flight response. The response induces stress or related states of mind. Thus, this is a fast way of easing conditions of anxiety. You can also do visualization exercises with your breath, imagining the air flowing in to be one color and the stress in your body (assigned a different color) to flow out when you exhale. The mind is a potent weapon for calming yourself down. Exercises as simple as color visualization can have a speedy effect when you are angry, frustrated, confused, overwhelmed, grieving, or other emotions.

Breathwork can also be accompanied by a mantra or affirmations. Chant these things in your mind or verbally so that they sink into the functioning of the unconscious mind. Further, chanting can have a relaxing feeling because of the rhythmic and slightly hypnotic nature it has. An alternative you can do is to breathe deeply and control the length of your inhalation and exhalation. Count to four slowly while you inhale, ensuring you are using your diaphragm and that the air fills you until your belly raises. After this, you can either breathe out fast and force the air to leave your body or count to six and breathe out slowly. Both techniques have the effect of lifting you, just in different ways.

The 5 Pillars of Mental Performance

Some tips to help you find the perfect affirmation for your breathwork practice include:

1. **Consider your current mindset and goals.** Think about what you want to achieve through your breathwork practice. What do you want to focus on or manifest in your life? Choose an affirmation or mantra that aligns with your current mindset and goals.

2. **Choose a positive statement.** Your mantra should be a positive statement that helps you feel empowered and uplifted. Avoid negative self-talk or words that focus on what you do not want.

3. **Keep it simple.** Choose a short and simple affirmation or mantra that is easy to remember and repeat. This will help you stay focused and present during your breathwork practice.

4. **Use present tense.** Write your affirmation in the present tense as if you are already experiencing the state you want to achieve. This way, you will make it more real and powerful.

Getting space is another way to help yourself build mindfulness. One method is to walk and observe all the senses you can about your environment. Bring yourself to the present moment. Another approach is finding somewhere to sit with pleasant scenery and observe what is happening. A coffee shop is a fun location to grab a seat and watch the back and forth of the public. You can see people in all states of mind, from flustered to bored, while you are sitting there relaxing with a warm beverage. Remain in the present and focus on the people around you, putting your phone on silent and ignoring the drama or demands of your day for a few minutes. You will feel calmer when you return to what you did after the sit-down.

A level up from taking a walk is doing a nature walk. In this case, you find somewhere with great natural scenery and soak in its beauty. You should remove your shoes to ground yourself onto the planet if it is safe. Putting your phone on do not disturb mode or leaving it behind will allow you to observe what is around you without distractions. Look for things that inspire awe and that you appreciate for their natural beauty. Understanding how big nature is concerning your life is humbling and puts your problems into perspective. Then, when you feel like you are in the present and relaxed, it will be much easier to think about the emotional situations you are going through so that you can experience the feelings they bring up mindfully.

Self-Awareness

Self-awareness is the key to emotional agility because you first need to be in tune with yourself before you can understand your emotions. There are many trigger areas in our lives. To understand yourself better and manage your emotions, you must determine what areas of your life trigger you the most. Knowing what those areas are will show you where you are most likely to have emotional flare-ups, especially the stronger ones. It will also show you what areas you need to do the most work to develop coping strategies for managing emotional states.

One of the most effective strategies is meditation. Practicing meditation builds your capacity to accept your emotions, making embracing them easier. As such, it allows you to manage your emotions better, especially when it is inappropriate or too strong to exhibit a particular feeling. When faced with such a situation, you can use the acknowledgment followed by a focusing mechanism. This process involves recognizing the emotion and its related thoughts and returning your attention to the task. By doing so, you can better handle the situation with poise and composure, despite any internal turmoil you may be experiencing. However, the real power of this technique comes from the fact that it is not a form of suppression or denial of emotions. Instead, it is a tool that allows you to temporarily set aside the emotions and address them later when you have the space and time to do so. Hence, it trains your mind to accept and move on from emotions to improve self-awareness.

Counseling is another strategy for knowing yourself well. In this case, you are working with someone who built up experience and knowledge over years of education and practice. They understand nuances of the mind, and they are there with the express purpose of helping you. The techniques they know can be tailored to your personality and life situations, making them more effective. Use this setting to raise your awareness of emotions in a controlled way.

Expressing Emotions in a Healthy Way

Like it or not, your emotions need to come out; if they do not, they will fester and infect your mind in unhealthy ways. Four healthy techniques are noted in this section for you to face the emotions in as healthy a way as possible.

Talking to Others

Therapy is an excellent way to express your emotions and receive support from a dedicated professional. A therapist's purpose is to listen to you and provide solutions that can help you overcome emotional difficulties and disorders. Likewise, they offer a judgment-free environment where you can explore the underlying causes of your emotions and learn how to express them. With the coping mechanisms they have learned through rigorous training and work, they can equip you with several methods to improve your life's quality and emotional well-being.

Friends and family can also act as a support system when you need to talk. However, select someone who can provide you with a safe space to speak freely and would not try to make the conversation about themselves. Once you have found the right person, share what is on your mind and how you feel. A compassionate listener can lift you and provide the support you need to feel better. Additionally, speaking aloud and breaking down your thoughts in a conversational manner can help you examine your experiences objectively and gain a deeper understanding of them.

All in all, seeking therapy or speaking to someone close to you can benefit your mental health and emotional well-being. Choose someone who makes you feel comfortable, and do not be afraid to reach out and connect with those around you. Remember, there is always someone willing to listen and provide a helping hand.

Journaling

Journaling is a communication method that you can use to talk to yourself and work out what is going on in your mind. Building a habit of writing your thoughts is soothing since you are letting out your emotions and ideas. It can calm you down even when you are going through the most intense emotions. Moreover, it allows you to put a name to all your ideas and feelings, giving you more certainty about yourself and what you are going through. Regular journaling builds self-awareness by showing how your mind thinks and what patterns you use to process information. Writing down information lets you compare data from different times and find new solutions.

You can re-read the notes later to gain different perspectives on the same topics.

A mood journal is particularly influential for this purpose. You use this type of journal to write about the feelings you go through every day. The emotions, whether good, neutral, or bad, get written down and examined by you. You can see the effects of underlying circumstances or incidents on your mind and how you might respond to those triggers in a healthier fashion. Lastly, mood journals are great tools for building perspective on patterns of behavior.

Cry, if Needed

There are many times in our lives when nothing works; crying and letting out our pent-up emotions is all that helps. Crying releases the pressure you have built up in your mind from grief, anxiety, hate, confusion, or general overwhelm. Sitting there and letting out the tears allows you to accept that you have been affected by the incidents that induced the emotions and to process the stress caused internally.

One of the results of crying is that your parasympathetic nervous system is activated. This system controls your ability to sleep and is separate from the system that regulates your fight or flight response. In other words, when you cry, you release yourself from your fight mechanism and calm yourself down. Likewise, crying reduces distress, resulting in more calm. Further, it lets out both endorphins and oxytocin, which provides you with an emotional boost. It is not uncommon to feel a sense of well-being after crying and to feel better about life and the world.

Release the Tension

Tension from stress and emotions affects our productivity at work and in our life pursuits. For instance, when playing a sport, you feel the rush of exhilaration and the tension of your subdued nerves. When you have gone through trauma or built up much emotional baggage, it gets more challenging to face the uncertainty and let it out routinely. This pent-up pressure then holds you back, affecting the things you want to do, such as being successful in your sport. It may even cause pain or induce illness.

To release it, you can make use of intentional movement techniques. Intentional movement includes meditative walking, tai chi, shaking, dancing, belly breathing, qi gong, yoga, stretching, walking, and martial arts. The intentional movement engages your mind with a calm task that requires attention to your body, allowing you to release physical sensations and tender spots that might have built up. The tender areas often subconsciously store memories that have been incorporated into the body, causing dis-ease. These stored memories are one of the reasons why other therapies that directly address spots on your body, like acupuncture and massage, are so effective at relieving tension. Further, any signals that might have become trapped in the limbic structures of your brain or on your nerve channels are allowed to flow out and release.

Use the range of techniques classified under stillness as an alternative healthy expression of emotions. Stillness techniques include progressive muscle relaxation, breathing exercises, listening to relaxing music, meditation, sitting in nature, and practicing affirmations. They help ground you in the present, your body, and your environment. The distraction gets slowed down and bypassed, allowing you to focus on your inner world in a more focused manner. Hence, the things you have been holding up inside will be easier to let out and flow away.

Chapter 7:
Four Steps to Emotional Agility

The following four sections show the main steps for using emotional agility daily. While the previous chapter showed techniques you could use to improve different aspects of emotional agility, this chapter shows how the process of the emotional skill itself works.

Showing Up

The first step is to *face your emotions*. Facing them might not always be easy, particularly when they are embarrassing or irrelevant to the situation. There might be people around you that make you feel bad for having or showing emotions about a topic. Invalidating personal feelings is even more prevalent when you are part of a culture that considers it essential to remain separate from the world around you regarding your private thoughts or feelings, i.e., they expect you to come off as strong and unemotional.

Working in a corporate environment is often like this. You see clients who pay large amounts for the company's services. They expect five-star treatment, which they pay for. In the process, many clients think it is okay to treat you like scum. It is inappropriate to backchat the client, shut them down, or respond with sass. Doing so would be to the detriment of yourself and the company, but facing that you feel used or disrespected is better than bottling it up. While you should not necessarily act on them, knowing your feelings and why is good.

That said, you need to face them at some point, preferably sooner rather than later. Notice what your thoughts are so that you can determine what your underlying perspective is on the issue. Your thoughts influence your emotions, so knowing where your beliefs lie about the topic will help to clarify your feelings and why you have them. They will also explain your behavior because it results from your thoughts and emotions, whether conscious or subconscious. Showing up to the party by seeing your thoughts will clarify the best ways to alter your behavior to suit your values better.

When you have noticed your thoughts, feelings, and behaviors, the next step is not to judge them. Try to understand them, even if only at a cause-and-effect level. Part of showing up is showing up as yourself, which requires self-acceptance.

Stepping Out

Stepping out is where you step back from your thoughts, feelings, and behaviors once you have spotted them. Meanwhile, stepping back is an essential step of the emotional agility process that you use to gain perspective. With the understanding and acceptance you gained in the previous step, you could appreciate your personal experiences. Once you step back, the bigger picture shows how there may be more to the situation or trigger than you would initially perceive.

With the example of dealing with entitled corporate clients, stepping out is the next step after accepting that you validly felt disrespected.

After work or during your break, sit back and look at the unfolded situation. You might notice a few things, like incomplete forms, that upset the client. Knowing this, you can take positive action to correct your co-worker who failed to complete the paperwork. When they are corrected, you will face fewer angry clients regarding that issue. You might also empathize with the client, seeing they were taking out frustration on you rather than blaming you. Their conduct was inappropriate, but now you have a greater understanding of the whole context leading to their outburst.

Your emotions are not you but rather the way you experience things. This distinction lets you separate yourself and makes it much easier to move past a feeling. An analogy that shows this is when you are in a plane. The plane goes up and down, changes direction, and weathers the elements with you inside. You are going along with its motions but not the plane. You are separate from it and will disembark at the destination. Likewise, you run with your emotions and use them to get from one place to another. Still, you remove yourself from the feeling when an effect has resulted. It can be helpful to work this separation into your daily proceedings. You are not an angry, sad, or anxious person (as examples), but rather a person experiencing anger, grief, or anxiety.

Walking Your 'Why'

Once you have disembarked from emotion, the next step is to consider your course of action. You will need a good acquaintance with your values and goals to determine your action. Your values are the guiding principles that allow you to make decisions through life, while your goals are the things you want to bring into existence. One is a *"route"* or way of life, while the other is a *"destination."*

The emotions and thoughts you looked at in the *"showing up"* step above produce impulses concerning their stimuli. You would have seen the bigger picture in the *"stepping out"* stage, including the trigger and emotion. Now, determine how to incorporate your values into actioning your takeaway regarding the stimulus. For instance, if a family member kicked you out of an event because you have a different political opinion from someone, you might feel angry. Stepping out of the situation will validate your emotion. Appreciating it allows you to sit back and consider the context of the fallout—your family.

You will see how your values fit the situation by living your *'why.'* Suppose you are a person who values your family connection. In that case, getting upset and harassing the other individual might permanently damage your relationship with other family members. Yet, you might also be a person who values respect and justice, in which case you will still want to communicate with the other party to call out their conduct.

Subsequently, you could devise an approach in which you call up the family member who threw you out a few days later and say you would like to speak with them. Meeting in a public place will help force things to remain civil, allowing you both to communicate and work out your differences so that a similar incident does not happen. Aligning this with your personal goal of having a close extended family that holds regular get-togethers could lead to celebrating an event with everyone (including the person you had a falling out with) so that you can all enjoy each other's company by moving past any awkwardness.

Moving On

The final step is to move on now that you have worked out and implemented your action plan. There is no point in returning to emotions you have already worked through; they will only serve to come back to life and ruin any sense of calm you have achieved over the event. Instead, focus on your values and goals to keep your efforts robust. Doing so is how to move on for good.

Making small changes to your habits is part of the action step that will prevent triggering scenarios from recurring. Triggering developments often happen because we contributed to bringing them into being. In some cases, they happen because of external causes alone. In this case, our habits contributed to too strong an emotional reaction. Working on tweaking our habits thus assists in preventing things from happening in the same way in the future. So, in the example of the family member throwing you out of the get-together, the habit of talking politics contributed to the problem. As such, refraining from talking about politics with the family, or at least those who are against the type of discussions you have about it, will go a long way toward keeping things civil and pleasant in the future.

Suppose you find it difficult to see where your habits contributed to the situation. In that case, it can always help get an external viewpoint. Talking with one or two other family members will allow you to expand your point of view to include things they observed or felt about it all. With the expanded observation, you can determine whether there are habits out of line with your goal about this part of your life.

Besides that, your emotions indicate how it all aligns with your values. By noting them, you can work out many flexible approaches to the same problem and make decisions relevant to your sense of personal integrity while remaining faithful to your goal. Do this to balance your sense of right and wrong, your feelings, and what you want to accomplish.

Pillar 4: Mindsets

Your mindset is essential to keeping your life productive and successful. A healthy attitude is a dynamite that explodes your life into spectacular results.

Chapter 8:
Exploring Mindsets

In this chapter, we will explore what 'mindset' means. The exploration will include a look into why mindset is essential and the two main categories; *fixed and growth mindsets*.

What is a Mindset?

Your mindset is a determinant of your outlook and behavior. It is a mental attitude that results from your self-perceptions (i.e., how you see yourself), specifically how you perceive your mind to be oriented. For example, suppose you see yourself as someone dedicated to improving your living conditions and upskilling yourself. In that case, you are a person with a growth mindset.

The Impact, Importance, and Effects of Mindsets

Your mindset shows your orientation toward life's challenges. It gives insight into your limitations and what you can achieve and shows how to expand to reach more. So, when you have determined whether you have a fixed mindset about something, you can alter it to a growth mindset; seeing that it is a growth mindset already will allow you to reinforce your efforts towards improvement or continue as you are.

When you have an opinion about someone else's mindset, it can affect how you treat them. This reaction is most evident in learning environments. When someone is assumed to have a fixed mindset, you might not be willing to give them the same amount of attention or effort as other learners. This neglect happens when people are classified as dumb or not too bright, leaving their unexplored potential in the dust. The result is inequality in terms of treatment and attitude.

The brain can grow and change, but first, you must understand this to be the case and be willing to do something about it. Brain growth links to a willingness to go through processes to expand new neural pathways. While in others, it would start by showing them they can learn more and elevate, even if stagnation was their previous norm.

Once a person understands that any mind can grow and improve, it unlocks the door to learning achievement. Even those looked upon as underachievers, menial laborers, or unsuccessful students can upskill themselves. Upscaling skill improves resilience in pursuit of goals, efficacy, and passion.

Two Types of Mindsets

The two types of mindset are either fixed or growth. You can have a fixed or growth mindset about yourself in general. Likewise, you can have a fixed or growth mindset about different topics and pursuits. In this latter case, you have a *'mixed profile.'* Whatever the situation, you can alter it to either a growth mindset or an enhancement of your existing growth mindset.

Fixed

If someone has a fixed mindset, they believe their capabilities get programmed into them from the start and that their intelligence level would not change. This stuck view gives the dreary outlook that you cannot succeed in some aspects of life, no matter how hard you try. As such, you might stop trying to do something from the start and ignore any opportunities you believe will surpass your abilities.

Rather than working on expanding your skill base and the talents you have, you resign yourself to documenting your skill level so that you know what avenues in life to pursue and which ones to ignore. When you meet a challenge and you cannot overcome it, rather than trying to learn more about it and reattempting success with your expanded knowledge, you rationalize the failure with excuses. The result is that you give up on that department.

This is observed in childhood athletics. One or more kids have the mindset that they are not built for sports and will never achieve. With this mindset, they would not even try to participate. Thus, those few children precipitate a lack of achievement based on their behavior. If you do not get them out of that mindset, they will never participate fully. The trick is to break through this fixed mindset and transition them into a growth mindset.

A fixed mindset, as such, is a mindset that limits participation, effort, and achievement. It cuts you short and prevents you from being the person you can be.

Growth

On the other hand, a growth mindset is a perspective that you can always become more capable with something. You might already be skilled in an area, but nothing prevents you from gaining more skills. Continuous skill growth describes many of our top soccer players who, although already among the best in the world, will continue learning, watching playbacks of their performance, and training for higher achievement.

Regarding abilities where you feel you fall short, you know that some training or education can bring the skills you need. I have seen this in a few older individuals who initially knew nothing about cell phones and digital technology. Other individuals their age had resigned themselves to relying on others for technological needs and services, while these individuals put in the effort to learn. While they knew they were already retired and the skill areas were undeveloped due to being new, they read books and magazines. They took courses to gain this new area of expertise. Those individuals are now self-reliant and valued members of their social committees and civil governing bodies.

Using the same example of school-age athletics, we will look at kids with a growth mindset. There may be some children who are not particularly good at the sports you are doing with them, but you would struggle to find the ones with a growth mindset bringing anything but their best effort. These individuals understand that with practice, strengthening, stamina-building, and understanding the rules and some theory, they will achieve eventually. This may be in a few weeks or even a few years, but their enthusiasm remains, and their grit carries them through to accomplishment.

The 5 Pillars of Mental Performance

Your brains and existing talent are your starting point, but you can constantly improve and be better. Neural plasticity is a feature of the brain that, if tapped, can lead to a future of a lot more success than your wildest dreams.

Chapter 9:
Growth Mindset

A growth mindset is necessary to appreciate the improvements you can bring about in your capacities. Still, it is also important to know that while growth is always possible, sometimes it takes time. Further, it takes effort. Brain plasticity is a remarkable aspect of your thinking abilities. It would be best to dedicate time and effort to practice taking advantage of this ability.

What Does Having a Growth Mindset Mean?

The core of the growth mindset is believing you can learn to be more intelligent than you already are. You can gain knowledge and problem-solving skills, whether from books, videos, or other information sources, but you will also require practicing skills, faculties, and memory retention. The process might require much commitment, but the results will pay dividends.

For those already considered above average in intelligence, there is comfort in knowing that you can raise it to even greater heights. Many intelligent people run into the problem that they think they are smart and have been assigned this ability since birth. The problem is that they resign themselves to their existing capacity, believing it is fixed. A fixed view can be disempowering when trying to accomplish something of immense complexity and feeling like you cannot meet those challenges.

Due to fewer learning resources on highly complex issues, you might think it pointless to try elevating your knowledge about them. However, learning resources are always available in one form or another, such as by speaking with top experts in a field. Without informational materials, you can formulate your own by conducting rigorous research. There is always a way to gain more knowledge on a subject.

Dedicated efforts result in brain exercise. By exercising the brain, you make it stronger and increase its capacity. By repeatedly using the same new neural pathways, you ingrain them. Establishing new paths makes it easier to use them in the future, thus building effortless competence. The desire for challenge keeps you returning for more in this repeated process of learning new skills and creating new neural pathways. It makes you more resilient to failure because you build the habit of continually attempting to expand your capacities when faced with trouble.

Benefits of Having a Growth Mindset

A growth mindset is the only mindset that lets you see your failures for what they are and use them to learn from for the future. Such learning allows you to prevent a repeat of future lack of success. Avoidance of the subject wherein you experienced failure is only one type of approach, but this does not allow you to expand your mastery of that subject. Seeing where you fell short, examining it, and learning from it does, however, give you that chance.

The 5 Pillars of Mental Performance

The growth mindset is the foundation for learning-oriented behavior. This type of behavior prioritizes learning as a central feature of your life. You can learn to become a better partner, parent, child, and citizen. The attitude of a lifelong learner is always to know a bit more than they did before. This includes gaining knowledge about themselves and their personality.

With a mentality like this, you can grasp more success. You will know more than you did yesterday and more than you did a few years ago. Other people with fixed mindsets will have resigned themselves to how they are and what they have, and they will have stultified and would not aim to achieve higher. If you have a growth attitude, you can set an example to others about how they can learn and improve. In doing so, you will enhance your level of influence and respect.

In addition to achieving new things that you could not before, you will know how to approach other things you already do well differently. Doing so can make you more efficient and make your approaches more sophisticated. When you want to carry something out, you will have a bigger picture of what to do and how your action fits the bigger picture. The complex web of how things fit together will become more apparent, and you will feel like you understand that world better.

The summary of your benefits from a growth mindset is, thus, that you will learn more, achieve more, understand yourself and the world better, and have a more positive outlook on life.

How to Develop a Growth Mindset

Developing a growth mindset might be easier than you think. It starts with an intervention in which your attention is brought to the capacity of the brain to be exercised and become stronger. Understand neural plasticity as much as possible. The person should have a firm grip on the fact that they can be the agent of growth in their brain, so long as they dedicate themselves to the task. An intervention like this could replace a conversation, a lesson, a talk, or video sharing. So long as they understand that they can improve their mind's power, they can achieve results.

In the case of a tutor, for example, you can teach children that they can expand their mental capacities. Neural plasticity can be explained by describing the brain as a network of roads. The cars on the roads are the thoughts in the brain, and they travel along the big highways the most. The big highways are the neural pathways we use the most, while new neural pathways are made as dirt tracks when cars explore new territory. As the tracks are used more by other cars, they become more permanent. Eventually, someone makes a proper dirt road as homes are built in the area and a tar road when the level of activity demands it. Using this example, you can show kids that even something as permanent as the road system can be altered, just as their *"fixed"* abilities and ways of thinking about themselves can be changed.

Show a person they can exercise their brain. You are expanding the brain's capabilities and exercising the organ itself. To do this, practice new skills repeatedly and learn further information. The process is sped along by good physical health, as your body (specifically your brain) does better when given the necessary resources. You can even expand the capability of the mind to assimilate information, which makes the learning process faster.

The 5 Pillars of Mental Performance

Study skills training is the next step toward building a growth mindset. Knowing that you can learn about anything is okay, but what if you do not know how to learn? Several courses teach you how to assimilate information well to understand new information for use. Looking online for information about studying effectively is one of the most manageable steps to accomplish this, as there will be well-researched scholarly information about learning. Learn this skill of absorbing information well because it will be one of the most decisive factors toward your future success when adopting a growth mindset.

The approach to developing a growth mindset is, thus, simple. The first step is to make the person aware that expanding their knowledge and skill is possible. The second is showing them that they can exercise their brain and achieve their desired growth; it will require them to exercise the brain through learning and practicing things. The final step is ensuring they have a solid grasp of learning new information effectively and efficiently. When this is all done, your growth mindset will be firmly in place and ready for use.

Pillar 5:
Mental Toughness

Mental toughness is the capability to push through difficulties and materialize your intentions. It requires rugged drive and determination, as well as self-care and self-empowerment. The following three chapters will give you insight into what mental toughness consists of, how to use mental conditioning, and how to instill mental toughness.

Chapter 10:
What is Mental Toughness?

In this chapter, we will look at the definition of mental toughness, how it can improve your life, and the four C's necessary to be genuinely mentally tough.

Definition

The crux of the definition of mental toughness is that you show determination in the face of unpleasant conditions. As former Scottish Secretary of State Walter Elliot said, *"Perseverance is not a long race; it is many short races one after the other."* To be mentally tough, you must know enough about your why and the value of your work to be willing to get up repeatedly. You may be able to give excuses for not getting up, but you do not. There is more value in getting up and putting your shoulder to the wheel again than lying down and letting things happen.

Mental toughness is when you train your mind to be resilient to confront situations that require a lot of mental or emotional strength, followed by bouncing back. Perseverance is a toughness component because when you face repeated or enduring undesirable conditions, you exhibit bona fide toughness. Resilience, which refers to taking big problems in your stride and getting up again, is another aspect of toughness essential to successful living.

College graduates are mentally toughness exemplified. They face material they do not understand and social situations that are new to them. They might even move away from home, leaving the life they know behind. Despite this, they persevere through the information, assignments, and practice to build new understandings. Resilience is built when they fail tests or do not do well yet continue showing up to improve. In the end, mental toughness is ingrained, and recruiters know the person sitting across from them has enough fortitude to dedicate their energy to achieve a result over a long period.

When you are mentally tough, you know that there are expectations on you and that you will put in your maximum capacity to fulfill them. You believe you are resourceful and can make your decisions or targets come true. When others do not have high expectations from you, you show them you are capable. Do not be held back by negativity; use it to fuel by proving those opinions wrong.

As with significant problems, handle minor setbacks with buoyancy. The minor setbacks cannot tangle you up with annoyance because you have bigger things to focus on. You are optimistic, and the small negativities are irrelevant to your targets. Mental toughness is, thus, the state of overcoming big and small difficulties, whether from people or situations and overcoming them using your skill and positive self-confidence, resulting in achieving the goals you have set out to accomplish.

Benefits of Mental Toughness

Mental toughness serves to benefit both yourself and those who rely on you. Improvement in your well-being results when you have been mentally tough over long periods. You will improve your station in life concerning your financial well-being when you use mental toughness in the workplace. You will also enhance the state of your business, team, or social group toward target attainment. The repeated levels of achievement result in more self-confidence because you know you are capable. You generally start feeling better about yourself, hence your state of mental well-being.

Likewise, mental toughness means the stress in your life will affect you less. Repeatedly going through difficult situations and getting yourself to stand back up again desensitizes you to such conditions. It becomes second nature to act in a resilient fashion and to be mentally prepared for stress. Thus, when you encounter stressful situations, they are expected and seen as a challenge for you to prove yourself.

Besides that, mental toughness can alleviate depressive conditions. When you face your demons and expectations, they start wearing you down. A problem is only a problem so long as it is left unhandled. So, when you are in a depressive condition and feel like there is no hope in the world, or you will never feel better, mental toughness forces you to get up and bring your A-game despite it. By getting up when you feel like this, you sort out your triggers and your troubles. You also gain self-respect for getting up, despite feeling horrible, and, thus, start to feel better about yourself.

Your sleep quality will often improve when you use mental toughness. Sleep can be impacted negatively by a range of incomplete tasks. They pile up and take our attention, making it difficult for us to disengage. Better sleep will also have spin-off benefits, such as feeling more energetic. Not to mention, your productivity and mental state will improve because of it.

4 C's Model of Mental Toughness

These four points are the core of mental toughness. You can keep your mind tough enough to meet your challenges with them.

Control

In this context, it refers to how in control you feel about your life and yourself. Your emotions and thoughts form a part of it, and the action steps mentioned in the third pillar will assist in improving how much in control you feel of both. There is also the matter of feeling in control of the life you live and the choices you make. When your decisions determine what you will do, you are in control, but if everything in your life seems to be determined by others, then you would not be in control.

The capacity to keep anxieties in check is an essential factor of control. When using mental toughness, you will face many challenges that may seem beyond your capability. Adopting a growth mindset and overcoming your anxieties by remaining resilient through your challenges is the solution. You do not have to reveal your stress or emotions to others if you do not want to stay in control, so long as your outlet is healthy and results in better survival per your values.

The emotions of others can make it more challenging to be in control, mainly if they distract you from what you are trying to do. The way to get around this is to ignore the distractions as civilly as possible and dedicate your attention to what you are getting done. You cannot control how others feel about what you do, so if you live your values, keep the distraction of others' emotions out of your mind. If you live according to their feelings, you are not living your chosen life and letting them control you.

Having a good sense of control improves your self-image. The esteem you will grant to yourself will go up because of your discipline over your mind and body. When using discipline with your values, you will develop a firm idea of your identity and beliefs. One of the results is that you become more comfortable with who you are, which leads to relaxation about your personality. This further boosts your confidence and makes you feel more capable of getting things done—there is a knock-on effect.

Top athletes are the prime example. When they go to training every day, they ignore the pain and strain. Their diets may not always be the most enjoyable or per their preferences. If they have social engagements where they need to stay up later or drink a lot of alcohol, they say *"no,"* even if they want to participate. Personal control builds a positive self-image in many cases.

Athletes know they can manage how they feel and behave. They also inspire others with their dedication. When they retire from a sport, their confidence in getting things done spills over to their new pursuits. We all know of stories in which retired sports stars became successful businesspeople, and we will continue hearing similar stories. The years of hard work paid off, as they know they will achieve results in their new ventures, and their business partners know it too.

Your life purposes are linked with your ability to control. A basic description of the context is that when you feel like you are moving towards your objectives, you feel in control. You feel out of control when you are moving away from your purposes or not progressing in their pursuit. Having enough resilience to make things happen in line with your intentions while being resilient in the face of things that try to pull you off track is proper control.

You can use yoga, visualization, positive thinking and affirmations, and attention control to improve your sense of control. Yoga reduces stress and teaches you how to slow down your mind to focus on a few essential things at a time. Visualization allows you to work out what you want, to picture how it will feel to have it, and how to achieve it. Positive thinking and affirmations fill your mind with hope or expectation of improvement. Hence, you have reason to keep going, and attention control practices the capacity to direct where you want your focus to be. In doing so, it is easier to block out external stimuli.

Commitment

Commitment is the drive to remain focused on achievement. Despite obstacles, you have set your mind to something and will make it come to fruition. Dedication is a characteristic of a reliable person who will build others' trust in you. To make it easier to commit to a result, you must work out the end goal or target you are trying to achieve. You are working towards this goal, so if you have a clear picture, you will not fall into confusion and directionlessness. Consistency on the path toward that goal is something you can maintain without much difficulty.

A low level of distraction is one of the results of commitment because you are dedicated to achieving something specific and do not pay unnecessary heed to things that do not contribute. It becomes a habit to focus on success and growth rather than things that might drag you down or pull you away. This focus is one of the reasons why commitment is a component of resilience when it comes to mental toughness. With commitment, you are resilient in getting yourself back on track toward completing the tasks that are your responsibility.

Setbacks happen less because you are more likely to see them coming. After all, your attention is in the right place. That said, even when setbacks do happen, you are already in the habit of driving yourself toward your destination, so going through the lower gears after you have stopped to handle a barrier is something you would not mind doing. You know that you need to go through the lower gears before you get to the higher gears and speed toward your desires and needs.

A trick to make it easier to commit to things is to work micro-goals into your bigger plan. The daily to-do lists and production targets are tools you use to get smaller steps done that are necessary for getting more significant things done. Lay out the micro-goals so that they progress to the bigger ones. So, please do not make your daily goals without having your overall targets in mind. Otherwise, it is easy to become passionate about things that go nowhere or to use your energy enthusiastically toward things that would not advance your goals.

A last skill important for practical commitment is knowing how to prioritize. To work out priorities, you need to visualize the hierarchy of assignments and actions in terms of importance. When you put all your attention on things that are low on the scale of priorities for whatever reason (whether it be hobby horsing or being scared to look at something of a higher importance), then you are going to wind up with essential things becoming more and more of a problem. Reaffirm the most significant priorities to yourself and the benefits they will bring so that it does not become untenable to achieve complex priorities with built-in complexity.

Challenge

Seeing problems as challenges make life more fun. It also contributes to toughness, as the desire to dedicate effort is higher when solving a challenge that engages your life. Being driven to be your best causes you to operate at your most elevated level possible. See the challenge as an opportunity to prove your efforts true. You can gain something from overcoming a challenge, even if it is just personal pride at completing something difficult when others did not expect you could.

Change and variety are also opportunities to expand and use your mental toughness. The changes you face are challenges, and others might succumb when faced with them. We see this all the time with people after retirement who want to keep living the way they live or people of privilege who want to exclude others because it seems too complicated to allow change and variety.

But then, there are people like King Charles III of England who have enormous amounts of privilege and all the reasons in the world to prevent change from happening. Yet, he advocates for modernization and changing the English monarchy to suit the times. He formed the Prince's Trust to assist young people in grasping job opportunities, training, and education (especially those otherwise excluded from opportunities). He has used change as an opportunity to improve the lives of many people, even though others in his family or groups might have seen it as a threat to do so.

Using challenges to boost your mental toughness builds agility and adaptability. Fear of failure plays a minor role in your decisions and actions, while the drive for achievement plays a more vital role. Use your adversity as an opportunity to adapt, be agile, and come out on top. Often, life is unfair, yet feeling sorry for yourself and fearing that you will be subjected to more unfairness will keep you back. Even if you run into trouble, you will only surpass the injustice around you by adapting to the challenge and bringing about change yourself.

Confidence

Confidence, a trait you can develop, is an integral part of mental toughness. The attribute consists of believing in yourself and your capabilities to do what you set out to do. By having confidence, you will be more productive due to being less occupied with yourself and more occupied with your work. The level of productivity you accomplish and how capable you think you are playing a massive role in your confidence level. The more you can do, the more reason you have for self-respect and certainty in your ability to attain results. Education, training, and upskilling yourself are valuable contributors to confidence because of the nuance of result-attainment and skill capacity.

Your ability to influence others largely hinges on how confident you are. To engage others, you need enough confidence to communicate directly with them. Using your emotions, thoughts, and experiences to inspire, impact, and influence all require certainty. You would not be able to open up about yourself when you are too preoccupied with how others perceive you and lack the confidence to share yourself without too much of a filter. To have this confidence level, you must stiffen your resolve to deal with things coming at you, such as opinions, expectations, or countering efforts. Keeping your head, despite this, will help get your point across, and even if people do not openly admit it, they will respect you (even if deep down in a place they have never shared with you).

Confidence is a requirement to produce success. It allows you to take your setbacks when they come at you so that you get back up. A situation may be messy, and others with similar capabilities might not be willing to try to convert the mess into success. Still, when you have enough confidence, you will dive right into that mess and make the change others were unwilling to attempt. To generate this attitude of confidence, it helps to use imagery of your success, practice taking on more autonomy in your daily actions (to become self-reliant), and be willing to make mistakes and learn from them.

Chapter 11:
Mental Conditioning

Disciplining your mind to be more resilient in achieving your goals is what mental conditioning is all about. It requires dedication to your dreams because they provide the energy you need to keep going when it gets tricky. Mental conditioning requires continued effort, so the habits you want to build start sinking in. Your mind toughens up with the long-term commitment to conditioning your brain to be robust to avoid the old neural pathways that lead to laziness or other undesirable states.

Physical activity is an excellent way to condition your mind. You are putting yourself through difficult situations that tire you out and convince yourself there is a benefit in keeping going. Besides this, the exercise will relieve stress and help calm you down. Meditation and mindfulness practices are other ways you can condition your mind. Both teach you to slow down your thinking by filtering out distractions and remaining aware of the priority of the moment. Visualization also helps because you repeatedly show your mind what your goal is and how you will achieve it while also cutting out consideration of irrelevant things.

Mental Conditioning and Your Inner Strength

Conditioning your mind brings out the strength inside. The process shows you that you are challenged and that, with the correct input and practice, your mind has robust capabilities. Having strengthened mental faculties makes staying positive in the face of danger or opposition much easier. The circumstances do not influence you much because you are rugged enough to tolerate and thrive in them. Further, conditioning your mind allows you to keep going even when you do not have motivation.

All these books about finding meditation do have relevance. Sometimes, there is no motivation for something—no matter how hard you look. With conditioning, you rely more on your strategy and the habits you have ingrained in yourself. Thus, you can still get what you need without motivation.

Take the example of an entrepreneur. They have a vision of forming a business that sells water filters. They want to create the most successful water filter business in their city and make a large profit. As the years wear on, progress might not be as fast as they want. The whole endeavor might feel like a drag, but with mental conditioning, they keep showing up every day and making sales, no matter how demotivated they feel. They put on a smile and explain the benefits of their devices.

Eventually, their years of work pay off after forming a joint venture or partnership. The cash injection opens new possibilities, with the company expanding beyond their wildest dreams. A few years later, they sell off their share of the business, making enough money to retire. Without mental conditioning, this whole process would have proven futile.

The 5 Pillars of Mental Performance

The easiest way to condition yourself is to use activities and practices that expose you to challenges. The use of endurance in those challenges trains your mind to keep going despite the forces against you. Coming out stronger on the other side is inevitable since your brain is now more comfortable facing difficulties. It validates your capacity to work through messes through successful accomplishment. The practices you do to expose yourself to situations that are not easy can be real or imaginary. Imaginary ones still train your mind because you are learning to problem solve and persist despite difficulties—do this using visualization techniques.

Mental conditioning is an excellent way to improve self-control and the capacity to master your emotional expression. Sometimes, not expressing yourself is a more potent way to show mental toughness than to express yourself in the heat of the moment. Reacting civilly by being the better person or keeping your face focused when you are tired from physical exertion against the opposition on the field are instances when self-regulation shows mental toughness.

It shows awareness of your inner self along with the use of healthy coping mechanisms to master your reactions and let out your emotions maturely. You can, and should, still express your feelings, but do so in an appropriate format using practical means. It is much more lasting to submit a formal complaint about someone using civil language than to throw your toys out the cot and make yourself look like a fool.

Learning to calm down in heated situations is part of mental conditioning, especially in interpersonal relations. Using breathwork techniques to calm your mind and body is practical to subdue your strongest urges to explode. The process of handling situations effectively by conditioning your mind to respond in a refined way requires you to take a step back from the challenging situation, examine it (including the context), determine where the source(s) of the problem lie, and working out a plan to surmount those sources in line with your values. Doing so conserves your energy and results in more innovative solutions that are more effective (due to being properly thought out).

Talking to another person is an excellent way to process what is happening in your head. If you can find someone you trust, speaking with them will give you a better perspective on your situation and help you develop solutions. It also gets the whirlwind of thoughts and emotions to subside, making it easier to bring yourself to the present. In these conversations, it can be healthy to admit your mistakes and work out where your shortcomings were. When you do so, you allow yourself to grow from your errors because you have faced that mistakes exist. It also builds bravery because you have pushed your ego aside to be honest in a challenging situation.

Attention control exercises also help. Making yourself aware of what is happening around you using multiple senses helps bring your mind to the present. With more attention available to you in the present, you can direct your mind towards your intended destination and tasks better. You will be more aware of things that might cause a problem, allowing you to prepare better for them. Your mind, thus, gets conditioned to remain in the present to a large extent, to look out for potential problems that may arise, and to figure out a few solutions to face that problem head-on. The stamina of your mind will also be higher through all of this.

Arousal is another thing that needs to come under your firm grasp when conditioning your mind to become sturdier. Arousal refers to something that keeps your mind entertained and engaged. When your

The 5 Pillars of Mental Performance

mind gets used to high arousal levels, focusing or maintaining your composure for long periods becomes challenging. You have become comfortable sitting back and relaxing while hyperstimulation of your mental faculties occurs. Using progressive muscle relaxation, visualization, and mindfulness brings arousal to a level that is easy to control. This way, you do not have so little arousal that you are entirely disinterested. Still, you are also not so aroused that you cannot seem to focus on anything. A healthy middle ground is best.

Resilience

Resilience training can help you incorporate mental conditioning better. The quality of resilience allows you to change the conditions in your life, whether intricate or uncomplicated. Knowing your stress triggers is an excellent way to make yourself more resilient. The presence of stimuli in your life will continue from birth to death. Understanding the ones that set you off the most or to the most substantial degree shows what areas of your life you need to condition the most. Use of coping mechanisms and facing triggers head-on conditions you to remain unaffected by stimuli. You will start to feel better and more confident about your mental strength.

Resilience training teaches you how to find a balance between aggression and being passive. Being passive can be good in some situations, but only sometimes. On the other hand, aggression is a valuable state under your control, but once again, only a condition to be in some of the time. The flexible balance between the two is struck by building self-awareness and managing your emotions, reaction to stress, and problem-solving abilities. The process of training yourself to be more resilient starts with finding what your comfort zone is, following which you gradually expand it. Trying to face everything at once makes you despair or feel incapable. However, working on a continuous change brings about a gradual, comfortable expansion and results in confidence.

Comprehensive resilience training does not only incorporate working through challenges but also becoming more aware of your health (in both your mind and body). The stressors you face affect your body and require self-care to recuperate from. Your mind is also brought to lower levels by being worn out, subject to negative emotions, and being faced with complexities that are difficult to solve. Working through trauma is an integral part of improving your resilience levels because getting past the things that pull you down the most will make it easier for you to bounce back when you are down in the future—you are not driven into unresolved trauma each time. Lasting accomplishment is the effect of handling your whole self.

The way you do resilience training is to find something to do that you will find challenging. A challenge can be anything from learning a new subject to preparing for a marathon. These pursuits provide challenges that require you to set goals, acquire skills, and take decisive action. The journey teaches you about yourself in your journey of working out solutions. It develops a positive self-view when you see you are a capable problem-solver. You will learn that change is part of life and that you can use it as an opportunity rather than experiencing it as a catastrophe.

Some practices you can do to improve your resilience in addition to resilience training are meditation, journaling, doing spiritual or philosophical introspection into the change you want to bring into the world, and practicing gratitude towards yourself and others. Knowing that you can do something that improves the world is uplifting and provides a deeper drive than many other things.

A final thing you can do, although not a practice or activity, is build connections with people. They can provide you with new perspectives on the world and the challenges you face. They can also give you an example of how their effort and hard work have assisted them. These meaningful connections can have a beneficial effect on your resilience and mental toughness.

Mental Flexibility

Mental flexibility is necessary to run with all the changes and challenges you will face daily. To adapt and change, you must be flexible to think with variables. Remain fully in the present and run with your challenges by using your central values to accomplish this. Having the capacity to disengage from unimportant things or things that do not relate to the problem at hand is vital for compelling mental flexibility. Conversely, remaining engaged with multiple priorities at the same time while dedicating most of your effort and attention to the core task of the moment is just as crucial for mental flexibility. Doing this, you constantly create new synaptic connections and use neural plasticity, strengthening your brain.

As a result, you should be able to learn faster than before because you can picture new content and perspectives without trouble. The solutions you adapt to problems will also come to mind quickly and should, generally, be more creative than others without flexible minds. What will set you apart from your competition is that you are not stuck in your ways and can incorporate new technologies, developments, and competencies. At the same time, they may not be able to do the same.

To develop a flexible mind, try things like changing your daily routine or meeting new people. Getting different perspectives on morals from the people you meet can contribute to critical thinking and cultural respect. Reasoning with other moral systems contributes to healthier interaction and a more flexible social aspect while validating the core morals and ethics you live by through healthy debate or exchange. Further, new experiences can often be just as enlightening as new people. Going through new experiences enhances your understanding of the world and the people who live in it while also releasing dopamine, which results in better memory enhancement and learning motivation.

While gaining new perspectives, you should try divergent thinking to enhance the creativity with which you solve your problems. Divergent thinking is where you quickly generate as many ideas as possible, even if they are unrelated. Some of the concepts might not be workable, but others will be. Nevertheless, breaking down the barriers of rigidity in your mind leads to better out-of-the-box thinking in the future. As a remark, do not always look for an easy solution. Sometimes, there are more complicated solutions, but their results are more permanent and have a higher degree of positivity. Having the barriers in your mind broken down healthily also allows you to make connections between different areas of your existing knowledge that you might not formerly have noticed.

Chapter 12:
How to Build Mental Toughness

In this chapter, there will be explanations of the four main things you can do to formulate mental toughness. They will show you how to see challenges as opportunities and be flexible in pursuing them.

Connect to Your 'Why'

Your *'why'* is a profoundly personal thing you need to know before you have proper direction. It is the thing that ensures that the work you do matters and the goals you have are linked together. It is what you want to accomplish, be, or do that makes you want to get up in the morning. You might know what it is already, and it might take years to figure it out if you do not. One of the things you can do to figure it out faster is to set your goals with a long-term view. Those goals develop a sense of purpose and a future-oriented perspective on life. Plans help drive you to achieve, and finding how to get there becomes part of the fun.

You will need to take many steps to accomplish your goals in life. They might demand much exertion on your part. Knowing what your values are is an essential factor in proceeding through the underlying tasks toward your goals. Your purposes and values, when combined, help you make decisions quickly and with certainty. They also define who you are and what you want to accomplish. Due to the nature of values giving your central personality clarification, they make you flexible in your daily work as you have very little uncertainty about what actions are right for you to do—even in situations you have never been confronted with before.

Although an extreme example, patients who overcome terminal illnesses are one of the best embodiments of this. The process they went through was emotionally, spiritually, and physically taxing. A cancer patient going through radiation faces immense struggle every day. During this time, many patients re-prioritize what and who they consider important to them. They clarify their values and determine what they want out of life. Those lucky enough to overcome the illness often have a very strong sense of personal identity due to the introspection they underwent. Afterward, they process decisions quickly, knowing what actions align with their values and what they want from life.

The same goes for situations that comprise much pressure. Those situations might demand you to make fast decisions based on little information, but with your guiding values, you will see what decisions would be out of the question and what to stand by roughly. Thus, values and goals contribute to determining your *'why'* in life—values give you an identity and path to follow daily, and dreams provide a long-term view.

Knowing what matters to you further assists in concluding your *'why'* because it shows what you care about. Josephine Perry (2021) proposes going through your phone's gallery and seeing what pictures you have taken and downloaded to see if there are central themes. Those major themes suggest deeper meanings you can use to see your *'why.'*

The 5 Pillars of Mental Performance

Let Go of Self-Limiting Beliefs

The person who knows you the best is often yourself. You know what you do well and where you fall short. Often people focus on their shortcomings and lose sight of where they shine. It is sometimes popular for people to say things like, *"I am dumb," "I am so clumsy,"* or *"That is just me,"* with negative connotations to elicit a laugh or make themselves more relatable. Doing this does not contribute to building self-confidence and achieving in this world. Rather than highlighting your limits, acknowledge them and focus on your abilities.

Life has a lot of stress for everyone. There are problems, hardships, setbacks, and a whole range of other things we do not want to experience. Often, the negative things people go through are unfair, and they cannot help but feel overwhelmed, or like they did something wrong to deserve their difficulties. If you have thoughts like this, do not go down the spiral of validating them. Acknowledge those thoughts, then change the way you think about them. Increase your vocabulary of emotions so that you can describe the feelings with those thoughts exactly, then use those emotion labels to disengage and become more objective about the negative emotions.

Start looking at the bigger picture, wherein you realize that single thoughts and incidents can cause you to tumble down but that there is so much space to get back up and succeed despite failure. Do not fear failure or perceived inadequacy; instead, focus on what you can achieve with the attributes you do have. Learn how to use tactics to be tougher to solve your problems better. By solving your problems, you will regain the self-trust needed to mold a healthy self-image. You are in control of the trajectory of your life a lot more than most people.

There may be some who can exert much influence on what becomes of you, but you are still the central character in your story. See how you can control your decisions, positivity, and personality to cut short the limitations you put on yourself and lift yourself.

Overcoming Self-Doubt and Negative Self-Talk

Reframing negative thoughts brings about immense relief and contributes to mental toughness. Isolate the ideas in your mind that bring about self-doubt or break you down. Write them down and see them sitting before you, noting that they are now on paper rather than in your head. Go through each one and work out how to rephrase it to be empowering or have a positive effect. A thought like, *"I struggle to talk to people,"* can be altered to, *"I had trouble talking to Joe because I know the value of being perceived well."*

Another approach is to think of those thoughts being said in funny voices or by comical characters. Throwing humor into the situation makes the ideas less severe, which, in turn, helps elevate you out of the quagmire they have created in your mind. Alternatively, you can rephrase the thoughts in the third person. If you thought, *"I am ugly,"* then you can change it to, *"[your name] had the thought that they were ugly."* This phrasing acknowledges that it was a thought and nothing more and allows you to distance yourself from the statement in the same breath.

Further, if you say something self-deprecating in a high-pressure situation, realize that what a person says when under much strain is often exaggerated. The classic example is the sales manager telling their employees they are useless and do not deserve their pay when the sales manager's job is on the line for departmental underperformance. This statement could be very far from the truth. Yet, the employee sits there with this exaggerated statement that does not consider all the targets they have met and the extra work they put in beyond their job specification. The same applies to things you say to yourself under pressure—they are often exaggerated.

Solution-based thinking is the remedy if you are having thoughts about anxiety and fear. They move you past avoidance and engage your mind in tackling the situation. Thus, you feel like you can cause change to the problem, which empowers you as a person. Focusing on overcoming the stress, rather than the feelings you are going through due to the pressure, will lead to outcomes and moving past harmful thinking mechanisms.

Visualization

Visualization is empowering and has advancing qualities in multiple pillars of this book. Nowhere is this clearer than in building mental toughness. The approach, however, is entirely different from how you use the exercise in other pillars. When you visualize to make yourself tougher, you need to picture difficult situations that you are in. The conditions should preferably be relevant to the struggles you face or will face while striving towards your goals so that the exercise is as appropriate as possible.

Once you have visualized the situation well enough with all the perceptions you can think of, work out different approaches to moving past that situation. This process generates solutions, paths for advancement, and confidence to escape the situation. You will come at the problem a lot more prepared when you face it in real life because you have already pictured it, along with a range of strategies to overcome it. When you do the visualizations, make sure that you also imagine yourself victorious, along with the sensations and feelings you will feel once you successfully surmount the challenge. The visualized goal gives you an end goal for the situation. Hence, you have something immediate to work towards—the victorious surmounting of the problem.

There are other visualization techniques that you can use to improve mental toughness. Visualization of pleasant scenes will help keep you calm when facing something demanding. Another is a visualization practice proposed by Josephine Perry (2021). She suggests imagining yourself as a bus driver going down a road to a destination in the distance. The passengers on the bus are the negative thoughts and emotions you face daily, and the road is the values you use to guide your conduct and decisions. The destination at the end is the goal you are working towards. Hear the passengers' chatter and acknowledge them while focusing on moving down the road of your values. This exercise teaches that while negative thoughts and emotions exist, you do not have to let them distract you from achieving your aims. The toughness required to not succumb to their chatter becomes part of your character when you do the exercise often enough.

Doing frequent visualization techniques is the only way to make them count. They become ingrained in your habits, allowing you to remain tough despite opposition.

Conclusion

This book delved into deep topics. The topics covered relate directly to you, your future, and your success. When adhered to, the pillars will give you immense strength and capacity to pursue your dreams ardently.

The first pillar we covered was the foundation—cognitive performance. We examined what it is and how you require good mental performance in your daily pursuits. You will only be truly successful when you move past mere cognitive coping and functionality to perform at an exceptional level of effectiveness. The content of the following four pillars showed how to build on the performance of your mind and provided you with techniques you could use to enhance your mental potential.

The second pillar showed what thoughts are and why being in touch with yours is essential. Multiple aspects of the mind and thought process were examined, specifically at the power of cognitive distortion and negative thinking on your success. The mutual impact of thoughts and emotions was also looked into, showing that your thinking directly affects your feelings. When you master your thoughts and confront your emotions, you can process them better and use your emotions as catalysts for action.

The third pillar concerns your emotions and how to use emotional agility to guide your conduct. Using information from the previous pillar, we elucidated the link between your emotions and your *'why.'* Your values and goals directly interact with your emotions and thoughts, providing an interplay you can take advantage of. To do this, you need to be in tune with your emotional self through processes of gaining self-awareness and learning how to express your emotions in healthy ways; only then will you have the fortitude to use your emotions as an agile tool to get you closer to your goals.

In the fourth pillar, we examined the difference between a fixed and a growth mindset. The importance of a growth mindset was made clear, specifically regarding its impact on your life when you realize that you can gain any skill. You can improve any of your faculties. The power of neural plasticity is yet at the tip of the iceberg of exploration. Yet, neural plasticity has already clarified the influence your efforts towards knowledge and skill-gaining can have.

The final pillar, mental toughness, indicates that mental toughness is more than being rigid in the face of opposition. It also includes self-care and exploring your why, goals, and values. You will be more motivated to overcome hurdles when you have something to work towards. And when you have values, a sense of resilience, and a grasp of the process you are to follow, you will have the power to get up and achieve even without emotion. The result of achievement will help you gain a positive sense of trust in yourself and your abilities, and the validation of your abilities will toughen you up in the face of future challenges.

In this book, you saw how you could directly impact your performance as an individual. You gained solutions and examples about controlling yourself and doing better in your tasks. You are the lead character in your story, and what you do to improve your knowledge and capabilities matters.

Glossary

Analytical: Having the quality of detailed examination.

Awareness: Knowledge about something that is happened or about something that exists.

Cognition: Processing information and signals that can be used for reasoning.

Cope: To overcome or manage a situation or problem.

Grasp: To understand something fully.

Gut feeling: An instinctual understanding or emotional reaction to something that usually happens instantly beneath your level of awareness.

Healthful: Good for your mind or body's condition.

Imagination: The mental faculty of forming things in the mind that are not present or do not exist.

Introspection: Examining yourself, whether emotionally or about your thoughts.

Manage: To deal with something successfully or in a way that promotes survival.

Morals: Standards of behavior you follow about what is right and wrong.

Pleasure: A feeling of enjoyment or having obtained the desired result.

Reflection: Thinking deeply about something.

Rumination: Repeated, deep thinking about a specific topic.

Snap judgments: Deciding quickly or instantaneously.

Stimuli: Things that you perceive in the environment.

Tough: Remaining strong or intact despite pressure, difficulty, or pain.

Values: The standards or behaviors you judge as important.

References

Ackerman, C. E. (2019). What are positive and negative emotions and do we need both? (W. Smith, Ed.). *Positive Psychology.* https://positivepsychology.com/positive-negative-emotions/#both

Analytical. (n.d.). *Merriam Webster.* https://www.merriam-webster.com/dictionary/analytical

Anzilotti, A. W. (2019, February). *Dealing with stress in sports.* Nemours TeensHealth. https://kidshealth.org/en/teens/sports-pressure.html#:~:text=To%20keep%20stress%20levels%20down

Awareness. (n.d.). *Merriam Webster.* https://www.merriam-webster.com/dictionary/awareness

Bedsworth, J. (2022). How emotional agility can help you make decisions and reach your goals (M. Bapat, Ed.). *GoodRx.* https://www.goodrx.com/health-topic/mental-health/how-to-practice-emotional-agility

Boaler, J. (2013). Ability and mathematics: the mindset revolution that is reshaping education. *Forum,* 55(1), 143. https://doi.org/10.2304/forum.2013.55.1.143

Briggs, S. (2014). *30 ways to inspire divergent thinking.* InformED. https://www.opencolleges.edu.au/informed/features/divergent-thinking/

Burgess, L. (2017). Eight benefits of crying: Why it is good to shed a few tears (T. J. Legg, Ed.). *Medical News Today.* https://www.medicalnewstoday.com/articles/319631#why-do-people-cry

Casablanca, S. S. (2021). 9 tips to change negative thinking (K. Gepp, Ed.). *Psych Central.* https://psychcentral.com/lib/fixing-cognitive-distortions#change-roles

Chadwick, J. (2020). Going on a 15-min "awe walk" each week and stopping to appreciate nature helps boost positive emotions and reduce stress, study shows. *Mail Online*. https://www.dailymail.co.uk/sciencetech/article-8756431/15-minute-awe-walks-nature-boost-emotional-being.html

Chapter 9: Remembering and judging. (2014). *In Introduction to psychology: First Canadian edition*. BC Campus. https://opentextbc.ca/introductiontopsychology/chapter/8-1-memories-as-types-and-stages/

Cherry, K. (2023). What is classical conditioning? (S. Gans, Ed.). *Verywell Mind*. https://www.verywellmind.com/classical-conditioning-2794859

Cherry, K. (2023b, February 27). The unconscious mind, preconscious mind and conscious mind (S. Gans, Ed.). *Verywell Mind*. https://www.verywellmind.com/the-conscious-and-unconscious-mind-2795946

Cognition. (n.d.). *Merriam Webster*. https://www.merriam-webster.com/dictionary/cognition

Cognitive functions. (n.d.). Neuron Up. https://neuronup.us/areas-of-intervention/cognitive-functions/

Cohn, P. (n.d.-a). *How pro athletes deal with pressure*. Peak Performance Sports. https://www.peaksports.com/sports-psychology-blog/how-pros-learn-to-deal-with-pressure/

Cohn, P. (n.d.-b). *Mental toughness in pressure situations*. Peak Performance Sports. https://www.peaksports.com/sports-psychology-blog/mental-toughness-in-pressure-situations/#:~:text=Mental%20toughness%20helps%20you%20push

Cohn, P. (n.d.-c). *Sports visualization for athletes*. Peak Sports. https://www.peaksports.com/sports-psychology-blog/sports-visualization-athletes/#:~:text=Visualization%20in%20sports%20or%20mental

Cope. (n.d.). *Merriam Webster*. https://www.merriam-webster.com/dictionary/cope

Cronkleton, E. (2022). 10 breathing techniques for stress relief and more (C. Crumpler, Ed.). *Healthline*. https://www.healthline.com/health/breathing-exercise#takeaway

The 5 Pillars of Mental Performance

David, S. [Host]. (2016). Building emotional agility (Episode 453) [Audio podcast episode]. In *HBR IdeaCast*. Harvard Business Review. https://hbr.org/podcast/2016/09/building-emotional-agility

Developing mental toughness. (n.d.). Mental Toughness Partners. https://www.mentaltoughness.partners/developing-mental-toughness/

Dougherty, E. (2011). *What are thoughts made of?* MIT School of Engineering. https://engineering.mit.edu/engage/ask-an-engineer/what-are-thoughts-made-of/

Duszynski-Goodman, L. (2022). What does a mental health counselor do? (R. T. Spann, Ed.). *Forbes Health*. https://www.forbes.com/health/mind/what-is-a-mental-health-counselor/

Fabio, R. A., Caprì, T., & Romano, M. (2019). From controlled to automatic processes and back again: The role of contextual features. *Europe's Journal of Psychology*, 15(4), 773–788. National Library of Medicine. https://doi.org/10.5964/ejop.v15i4.1746

Falde, N. (2021). *Beginners guide to understanding the cognitive functions* (S. Melandy, Ed.). Truity. https://www.truity.com/blog/beginners-guide-understanding-mbti-cognitive-functions

Fowler, P. (2022). *Breathing techniques for stress relief* (N. Ambardekar, Ed.). WebMD. https://www.webmd.com/balance/stress-management/stress-relief-breathing-techniques

Gelles, D. (n.d.). How to meditate. *The New York Times*. https://www.nytimes.com/guides/well/how-to-meditate

Gill, B. (2017, June 22). New to visualization? Here are five steps to get you started. *Forbes*. https://www.forbes.com/sites/bhaligill/2017/06/22/new-to-visualization-here-are-5-steps-to-get-you-started/?sh=168802cf6e3f

Grasp. (n.d.). *Merriam Webster*. https://www.merriam-webster.com/dictionary/grasp

Grinspoon, P. (2022). How to recognize and tame your cognitive distortions. *Harvard Health Publishing*. https://www.health.harvard.edu/blog/how-to-recognize-and-tame-your-cognitive-distortions-202205042738

Gut. (n.d.). *Merriam Webster*. https://www.merriam-webster.com/dictionary/gut

Healthful. (n.d.). *Merriam Webster.* https://www.merriam-webster.com/dictionary/healthful

Horiuchi, S., Aoki, S., Takagaki, K., & Shoji, F. (2017). Association of perfectionistic and dependent dysfunctional attitudes with subthreshold depression. *Psychology Research and Behavior Management,* 2017(10), 271–275. Dove Press. https://doi.org/10.2147/prbm.s135912

How to build mental toughness through mental conditioning. (2022, December 1). Daniel Domaradzki - Power Performance. https://primexaos.com/how-to-build-mental-toughness-through-mental-conditioning/

How to look after your mental health using exercise. (n.d.). Mental Health Foundation. https://www.mentalhealth.org.uk/explore-mental-health/publications/how-look-after-your-mental-health-using-exercise

Identifying negative automatic thought patterns. (n.d.). Stress and Development Lab. https://sdlab.fas.harvard.edu/cognitive-reappraisal/identifying-negative-automatic-thought-patterns

Imagination. (n.d.). *Merriam Webster.* https://www.merriam-webster.com/dictionary/imagination

Introspection. (n.d.). *Merriam Webster.* https://www.merriam-webster.com/dictionary/introspection

Intrusive thoughts and how meditation can help. (2022, May 13). BetterSleep. https://www.bettersleep.com/blog/intrusive-thoughts-and-how-meditation-can-help/

Ishler, J. (2021). How to release "emotional baggage" and the tension that goes with it (J. Litner, Ed.). *Healthline.* https://www.healthline.com/health/mind-body/how-to-release-emotional-baggage-and-the-tension-that-goes-with-it

Lawson, K. (n.d.). *What are thoughts & emotions?* (A. Georgiou, K. Hathaway, & S. Towey, Eds.). Taking Charge of Your Health and Well-being. Retrieved March 8, 2023, from https://www.takingcharge.csh.umn.edu/what-are-thoughts-emotions

Learning to label my emotions. (n.d.). Habits for Well-Being. https://www.habitsforwell-being.com/learning-to-label-my-emotions/#:~:text=What%20is%20Affect%20Labelling%3F

Levinson, D., & Pfister, G. (2016). Mental conditioning. *Berkshire Encyclopedia of World Sport* (3rd ed.). Berkshire Publishing Group; Oxford Reference. https://www.oxfordreference.com/display/10.1093/acref/9780190622695.001.0001/acref-9780190622695-e-180;jsessionid=F18002CB6D63869BE7F4B7717B-33466F#:~:text=Mental%20conditioning%20involves%20disciplining%20the,countries'%20success%20in%20the%20Olympics.

Luenendonk, M. (2019). *Classical conditioning: Learn how to create habits for success*. Cleverism. https://www.cleverism.com/classical-conditioning/

Lyons, P. (n.d.). *The 4 C's of mental toughness*. Ambition. https://www.ambition.co.uk/blog/2017/02/the-4-cs-of-mental-toughness?source=google.com

Lyubomirsky, S., Sheldon, K. M., & Schkade, D. (2005). Pursuing happiness: The architecture of sustainable change. *Review of General Psychology*, 9(2), 111–131. https://doi.org/10.1037/1089-2680.9.2.111

Ma, W. (2016). Mind games: Exploring and analyzing the mind of an athlete. *The People, Ideas, and Things (PIT) Journal*. https://pitjournal.unc.edu/article/mind-games-exploring-and-analyzing-mind-athlete

Malve, H. O. (2018). Sports pharmacology: A medical pharmacologist's perspective. *Journal of Pharmacy and Bioallied Sciences*, 10(3), 126. https://doi.org/10.4103/jpbs.jpbs_229_17

Manage. (n.d.). *Merriam Webster*. https://www.merriam-webster.com/dictionary/manage

Mark Hyman, MD. (2020). *What is emotional agility?* [Video]. In YouTube. https://www.youtube.com/watch?v=h3wVJGJUBDw

Meek, W. (2013). How to understand your mind (E. Hagan, Ed.). *Psychology Today*. https://www.psychologytoday.com/za/blog/notes-self/201303/how-understand-your-mind

Breaking the cycle: Negative thought patterns. (2021, November 19). Sage Neuroscience Center. https://sageclinic.org/blog/negative-thoughts-depression/#:~:text=Negative%20thought%20patterns%2C%20or%20cognitive

Mental toughness: The key to athletic success. (n.d.). Trine University. https://www.trine.edu/academics/centers/center-for-sports-studies/blog/2021/

mental_toughness_the_key_to_athletic_success.aspx#:~:text=In%20
sport%2C%20mental%20toughness%20is

Mindsets. (n.d.). ReachOut. https://schools.au.reachout.com/articles/mindsets

Morals. (n.d.). *Merriam Webster*. https://www.merriam-webster.com/dictionary/morals

Morin, A. (2015). 7 ways people with phenomenal mental toughness fight stress. *Inc.Africa*. https://incafrica.com/library/amy-morin-7-ways-mentally-strong-people-handle-stress-effectively

Muck, P. (2021). *The benefits of yoga: How it boosts your mental health*. Houston Methodist Leading Medicine. https://www.houstonmethodist.org/blog/articles/2021/sep/the-benefits-of-yoga-how-it-boosts-your-mental-health/#:~:text=As%20a%20form%20of%20low

My top 10 perseverance quotes. (n.d.). Identity. https://identityglobal.com/my-top-10-perseverance-quotes/

Natarelli, M. (n.d.). How emotion drives brand choices and decisions. *Branding Strategy Insider*. https://brandingstrategyinsider.com/how-emotion-drives-brand-choices-and-decisions/#:~:text=We%20now%20know%20that%20up

Neale, P. (2022). Emotional agility: Giving you the power to choose. *Forbes*. https://www.forbes.com/sites/forbescoachescouncil/2022/10/18/emotional-agility-giving-you-the-power-to-choose/?sh=427c6c643507

Nihilism. (2023). In A. Augustyn (Ed.), *Encyclopædia Britannica*. https://www.britannica.com/topic/nihilism

Nunez, K. (2020). The benefits of guided imagery and how to do it (A. Klein, Ed.). *Healthline*. https://www.healthline.com/health/guided-imagery

Performance anxiety. (2019). GoodTherapy. https://www.goodtherapy.org/blog/psychpedia/performance-anxiety

Perry, J. (2021). How to perform well under pressure. *Psyche.co*. https://psyche.co/guides/how-to-perform-well-under-pressure-by-cultivating-flexibility

Pleasure. (n.d.). *Merriam Webster*. https://www.merriam-webster.com/dictionary/pleasure

The 5 Pillars of Mental Performance

Positive thinking: Stop negative self-talk to reduce stress. (2022, February 3). Mayo Clinic. https://www.mayoclinic.org/healthy-lifestyle/stress-management/in-depth/positive-thinking/art-20043950

Priming. (n.d.). *Psychology Today*. Retrieved March 1, 2023, from https://www.psychologytoday.com/za/basics/priming

Raglin, J. S. (2001). Psychological factors in sport performance. *Sports Medicine*, 31, 875–890. Springer Link. https://doi.org/10.2165/00007256-200131120-00004

Raypole, C. (2020a, April 28). How to become the boss of your emotions (J. Litner, Ed.). *Healthline*. https://www.healthline.com/health/how-to-control-your-emotions#regulate

Raypole, C. (2020). Positive affirmations: Too good to be true? (M. A. White, Ed.). *Healthline*. https://www.healthline.com/health/mental-health/do-affirmations-work

Reflection. (n.d.). *Merriam Webster*. https://www.merriam-webster.com/dictionary/reflection

Ribeiro, M. (2019). How to be mentally strong: 14 ways to build mental toughness (S. Latif, Ed.). *Positive Psychology*. https://positivepsychology.com/mentally-strong/#:~:text=Think%20Positively

Roberts, A. (2022). *Emotional agility – Lean into the tough emotions* [Post]. LinkedIn. https://www.linkedin.com/pulse/emotional-agility-lean-tough-emotions-andy-roberts-/

Roncero, A. (2021). *Automatic negative thoughts: How to identify and fix them.* BetterUp. https://www.betterup.com/blog/automatic-thoughts

RSA. (2016). *Susan David on emotional agility* [Video]. YouTube. https://www.youtube.com/watch?v=0_6hu6JLH98

Rumination. (n.d.). *Merriam Webster*. Retrieved April 5, 2023, from https://www.merriam-webster.com/dictionary/rumination

RuPaul's Drag Race [@RuPaulsDragRace]. (2013). *If you cannot love yourself, how in the hell you gonna love somebody else? Can I get an amen? -_@RuPaul #DragRace #Wisdom* [Tweet]. Twitter. https://twitter.com/RuPaulsDragRace/status/298626899360505856?lang=en

Seladi-Schulman, J. (2018). Understanding explicit memory (T. J. Legg, Ed.). *Healthline*. https://www.healthline.com/health/explicit-memory#explicit-vs-implicit-memory

7 examples of classical conditioning in everyday life. (n.d.). StudiousGuy. https://studiousguy.com/classical-conditioning-examples-everyday-life/

Sieck, W. (2021). *Dual process theory: Two ways to think and decide*. Global Cognition. https://www.globalcognition.org/dual-process-theory/

Smith, M. (2020). The 6 habits of buoyant people. *Medium*. https://psychologymarc.medium.com/the-6-habits-of-buoyant-people-75cb05c0fac2#:~:text=Buoyancy%20is%20a%20type%20of%20resilience%20specific%20to%20low%2Dlevel

Snap judgement. (n.d.). *Merriam Webster*. https://www.merriam-webster.com/dictionary/snap%20judgment

Solis-Moreira, J. (2023). 6 ways to practice self-love. *Forbes Health*. https://www.forbes.com/health/mind/how-to-practice-self-love/#:~:text=Self%2Dlove%20can%20be%20defined,of%20your%20overall%20well%2Dbeing.

Sports, drugs, and addiction. (2019). Gateway Foundation. https://www.gateway-foundation.org/addiction-blog/athletes-drug-abuse/#:~:text=The%20most%20recent%20research%20from

Sports psychology: Mindset can make or break an athlete. (2018, July 5). Oklahoma Wesleyan University. https://www.okwu.edu/news/2018/07/sports-psychology-make-or-break/

Stenger, M. (2017). *7 ways to develop cognitive flexibility*. InformED. https://www.opencolleges.edu.au/informed/features/7-ways-develop-cognitive-flexibility/

Stimuli. (n.d.). *Merriam Webster*. https://www.merriam-webster.com/dictionary/stimuli

Sundgot-Borgen, J., & Torstveit, M. K. (2004). Prevalence of eating disorders in elite athletes is higher than in the general population. *Clinical Journal of Sport Medicine*, 14(1), 25–32. https://doi.org/10.1097/00042752-200401000-00005

10 ways to practice positive self-talk. (2021, April 23). Delaware Psychological Services. https://www.delawarepsychologicalservices.com/post/10-ways-to-practice-positive-self-talk

The 5 Pillars of Mental Performance

The Dharma Coach. (2016). *What are "positive" emotions? Learn how to move into an emotion to create satisfactory results* [Video]. YouTube. https://www.youtube.com/watch?v=ztEcxT9b5e4

The psychology of emotional and cognitive empathy. (n.d.). Lesley University. https://lesley.edu/article/the-psychology-of-emotional-and-cognitive-empathy

The School of Life. (2017). *How to process your emotions* [Video]. In YouTube. https://www.youtube.com/watch?v=b197XOd9S7U

Tough. (n.d.). *Merriam Webster*. https://www.merriam-webster.com/dictionary/tough

Understanding your thoughts. (2021, May 10). Erika's Lighthouse. https://www.erikaslighthouse.org/blog/understanding-your-thoughts/

Values. (n.d.). *Merriam Webster*. https://www.merriam-webster.com/dictionary/values

Van Overwalle, F., & Vandekerckhove, M. (2013). Implicit and explicit social mentalizing: Dual processes driven by a shared neural network. *Frontiers in Human Neuroscience*, 7. Frontiers. https://doi.org/10.3389/fnhum.2013.00560

What is mental training? (2020, February 19). Positive Performance. https://www.positiveperformancetraining.com/blog/mental-training-introduction#:~:text=Mental%20Training%20in%20athletics%20means

Whitbourne, S. K. (2012, May 19). The complete guide to understanding your emotions (E. Hagan, Ed.). *Psychology Today*. https://www.psychologytoday.com/za/blog/fulfillment-any-age/201205/the-complete-guide-understanding-your-emotions

Wieland, A. (2021, October 25). Sports psychologist talks athletes and mental health (G. Johnson, Interviewer) [Interview]. *Penn Today*. https://penntoday.upenn.edu/news/sports-psychologist-talks-athletes-and-mental-health

Wood, K. (n.d.). *The connection between thoughts and emotions*. Kamini Wood. https://www.kaminiwood.com/the-connection-between-thoughts-and-emotions/

Printed in Great Britain
by Amazon